CONTENTS

Introduction:

The following is an adaptation of a Step Study I did online in the summer and early fall of 2005.

I've been in OA since February 11, 1986. I started working the steps and lost weight, then relapsed, then lost weight, then relapsed.

Finally someone in the rooms confronted me (I'll talk more about that in Step 12) and I discovered a method of working the steps that has worked for me. I became abstinent, worked the steps, and achieved the miracle of being freed from the foods that used to beckon to me, being able to be around them, without wanting them. That has been true for me since about May 1, 1993.

It took me about a year, as I look back, to achieve a healthy body weight, and I've maintained that body weight since that time. In March, 2005, I began to lose more weight for reasons I'll talk about later.

This Step Study

Those of you familiar with the well-known AA team of Joe and Charlie will recognize much of what I say here, although I base this study on my own experience, of course.

Virtually all of this step study is based on what I have learned from the great AA speakers, Joe and Charlie, Roger, and Blaine D. from Winnipeg, Canada, and a lot of reading of AA history and experience. I don't think much of what I have to say is particularly original. I therefore want to acknowledge the teachings of AA and of those who have given their time and effort and experience to convey the message of recovery to those who still suffer.

This version is dated Friday, February 8, 2019.

Because this represents a merging of the teachings of many Big Book thumpers, including the AA speakers Charlie, the two Joes, Blaine, and Roger, it's not original. I've simply put together the thoughts of others from an Overeaters Anonymous perspective. The text is copyrighted only to make certain that it remains unchanged—not to prevent its use.

Therefore reproduction of this book is permitted if the text and this note remain unchanged and copies are sold at cost (fund-raising by OA Groups alone is acceptable); as well, "OA" or "Overeaters Anonymous" or the name of the author should not appear on any title page. As well, the title given should reflect that it is a personal interpretation of the Big Book's directions for compulsive eaters.

This is a work constantly in progress. Criticisms, suggestions, disagreements, comments are very welcome. Contact the author by going to www.oaabigbook.info, clicking on the top image, and then clicking on "here" in the sentence: "Comments? Questions? You can send an e-mail **here**."

The Big Book

OA stands for the proposition that the Twelve Steps give us freedom from the bondage of food. If the steps aren't working for you, then maybe you're not working the steps in a way that works for you. It might therefore be worth it to try the approach to the steps used in this step study, based on the Big Book.

The Big Book was written as a set of directions for doing the steps. It was aimed at those people who would not be able to meet anyone from AA, because at the time it was published AA was centered in New York City, and Akron and Cleveland, Ohio. So the Big Book was written as a do-it-yourself manual. As such it is a textbook—a book which contains valuable information to compulsive eaters.

It's not a perfect book, that's for sure. It was written by Christian male alcoholics who had found themselves in the gutter and had done a lot of harm to other people. It needs to be interpreted and applied for people who did not have their exact same experience, and it sometimes needs to be clarified because of its 1930s language. But besides its being a great inspirational and loving book, it is one of the greatest textbooks ever written, and I hope you'll join me in the study of its directions!

The basic outline of the Big Book's discussion of the Steps is as follows:

To help you in this Step Study, it would be useful for you to download certain documents and forms, including Step Four forms, used in weekend Big Book Studies done for many OA intergroups. They're also reproduced in this study.

You're welcome to download them and distribute them however you want. The Step Four forms and the Step Eleven form were drawn up by an AA Big Book thumper in Winnipeg, Canada, named Blaine, and OA owes him a debt of gratitude for allowing these forms to be used. They've been used by thousands of people with great success! The forms have been slightly modified from Blaine's originals with his permission. Howard W. of Minneapolis has reformatted the Step 4 and Steps 8 & 9 forms to allow them to be filled in on your computer using a PDF reader like Adobe or PDF-Xchange..

Included among the documents is also a Step Four Outline, which summarizes a lot of the concepts you'll find discussed in this study.

Go to

www.oabigbook.info

to download all the forms and get the latest version of this Step Study. This book contains many of those forms as well.

- Step One: "The Doctor's Opinion", part of Chapter One, "Bill's Story", most of Chapter Two, "There Is A Solution", and Chapter Three, "More About Alcoholism".
- Step Two: part of Chapter One, "Bill's Story", part of Chapter Two, "There Is A Solution", Chapter Four, "We Agnostics".
- Step Three: part of Chapter Five, "How It Works".
- Step Four: part of Chapter Five, "How It Works".
- Steps Five, Six, Seven, Eight, Nine, Ten, and Eleven: Chapter Six, "Into Action".
- Step Twelve: Chapter Seven, "Working With Others", and part of Chapter Eleven, "A Vision For You". Chapters Eight,"To The Wives", Nine, "The Family Afterward", and Ten, "To Employers", can also be read as containing discussions of Step Twelve, but I won't be dealing with them in any great detail.

A much more detailed outline of the Big Book is found in *A Schematic Outline of the Big Book* as found at **www.oabigbook.info** or in the Appendix to this book..

Questions

The questions at the end of each chapter in this Big Book Study were part of the format of the original online Step Study on which this book is based.

I hope they're useful questions. They are *not* intended, however, to be substitutes for actually doing the steps. Doing the steps is what the rest of this step study is all about!

Why use the Big Book directions?

If the way you work the steps has given you the recovery described by the Big Book, then why would you switch?

If, however, you are not free from the bondage of food, if food at times becomes attractive to you, if you're really white-knuckling it, then why not try the Big Book directions? They're guaranteed!

The Twelve Provocations

As I've been taught, the Big Book stands for the following concepts. Each one of them is controversial in some OA groups. They are simply intended to create some interest in what follows. They are not intended to be offensive, however.

1. I am a *recovered* compulsive eater, not a recovering one.

2. Abstinence is *not* the most important thing in my life without exception; the consciousness of the presence of God is.

3. Although a sponsor, if available, is very important for recovery, a sponsor is not *necessary* to recover.

4. You can recover in *weeks*.

5. The Tools of Recovery are *not* an essential part of the OA program.

6. You *don't* take Steps One and Two.

7. Steps Three, Six, Seven, and Eight, should *not* take a long time to get through

8. You *don't* make amends to yourself.

9. You cannot carry the message until after you have completed Step Nine.

10. Service is *not* slimming.

11. Food *can* be discussed at meetings.

12. Every person who wants to be a member of OA should know exactly what having "a desire to stop eating compulsively" means.

These "provocations" are explained fully, beginning at page 69.

Step One, Part One—the Allergy of the Body:

The Big Book's approach to Step One is what Dr. William Silkworth, the doctor who wrote the two letters found in The Doctor's Opinion, called "the double whammy".

Put simply, we have (1) an *abnormality of the body* (he called it an "**allergy of the body**") which means that once we start eating certain kinds of foods or indulging in certain compulsive eating behaviors we develop cravings which overpower us; and we have (2) an *abnormality of the mind* (he called it a "**mental obsession**") which means that even if we stop eating those foods or indulging in those behaviors, our mind persuades us that we can return to eating those foods and indulging in those behaviors.

Thus we can't stop once we start (the **allergy** that creates cravings), and we can't stop from starting again (the **obsession** that sends us back). We are thus in a vicious circle. That is the explanation for yo-yo dieting, and for all the despair that we bring to OA when we join.

It's often said that alcoholics can stop drinking but OAers can't stop eating. From the Big Book perspective, that isn't correct. Alcoholics *have* to drink, but they can't drink alcohol. OAers *have* to eat, but they can't eat the foods or indulge in the eating behaviors that create the cravings.

The main difference between the member of AA and the member of OA is that everyone in AA knows that alcohol is the ingredient that AAers can't drink, whereas in OA different people may have different foods they can't eat and different eating behaviors they can't indulge in. Part of the job of Step One is for each individual to figure that out for him- or herself.

Please read *The Doctor's Opinion*. It's found just before page one in the book, although different editions have different page numbers. I ask you specifically to note the following.

On page xxvi of the 4th edition (xxiv of the 3rd edition), the writers of the Big Book emphasize what they see in Dr. Silkworth's long letter that is important for AA.

> When I quote from the Big Book and omit some words, I don't put in the usual dots like . . .
> I think it'll be easier to follow. I also capitalize important words for emphasis.
> I urge you to read the original; don't take my word for it that I've quoted fairly!

My Problem:

The Physical Allergy:

An allergy is an abnormal physical reaction to something. In my case, it's my binge foods and my binge eating behaviors. Once I start eating my binge food or indulging in my binge eating behaviors, I find it almost impossible to stop eating it.

The Mental Obsession:

An obsession is an idea which takes control over all other ideas. In my case, if I've stopped eating my binge foods or indulging in my binge eating behaviors, my mental obsession gives me reasons to go back to eat the binge foods or indulge in my binge eating behaviors.

My problem in a nutshell—the addict's dilemma:

I can't stop once I've started. And I can't stop from starting again.

> In this statement he confirms what we have suffered alcoholic torture MUST believe—that the body of the alcoholic is quite as abnormal as his mind. In our belief, any picture of the alcoholic which leaves out this physical factor is INCOMPLETE.

On pages xxviii to xxix of the 4th edition (xxvi to xxvii 3rd edition), Dr. Silkworth talks about the allergy:

> The action of alcohol on these chronic alcoholics is a manifestation [symptom] of an allergy; [and the allergy is a] phenomenon of craving [which] is limited to this class and never occurs in the average temperate drinker. These allergic types can never safely use alcohol in any form at all. Men and women drink essentially because they like the effect produced by alcohol. The sensation is so elusive that, while they admit it is injurious, they cannot after a time differentiate the true from the false.

> To them their alcoholic life seems the only normal one. They are restless, irritable and discontented, unless they can again experience the sense of ease and comfort which comes at once by taking a few drinks, [which then develops] the phenomenon of craving.

On page xxx in the 4th edition (xxviii 3rd edition), Dr. Silkworth describes a spectrum of alcoholic types, ranging from the psychopath through to the manic depressive through to a person perfectly normal in all other respects. He says that their *only* "symptom in common [is that] they cannot start drinking without developing the phenomenon of craving."

The phenomenon of craving:

What is this phenomenon of craving?

A phenomenon is an unexplained occurrence. It is something that happens for which we don't have a clear explanation. We can describe it. We just don't know why it happens.

The phenomenon of craving is a craving that can't be explained. It just happens. There may be biological reasons for the craving, and we know that there's a lot of research on why some people become binge-eaters. But the concept of the phenomenon of craving puts the emphasis not on explaining it, but on making it obvious and powerful.

What "the phenomenon of craving" describes is an overpowering urge for more and more.

I can talk about myself in this connection. And the best way is simply to tell those parts of my story that illustrate the phenomenon of craving. In that way you can discover similarities. There will be differences—the foods and eating behaviors that cause my cravings may not be the ones that cause yours. But if you're a member, or a prospective member, of OA, I'll bet you've had the same symptoms!

First example:

This is really virtually all my stories.

My hand has food; maybe my hand is holding a fork or a spoon with food, or maybe it's just holding the food itself. The food could be buttered popcorn or potato chips or ice cream or french fries. My hand is coming to my mouth and putting the food in my mouth, and going back and getting more food and putting more food in my mouth, and that just keeps on going.

Meanwhile my mind is saying to itself, "I've got to stop, I've just got to stop. If I eat any more, I'll burst. If I get any fatter, I'll have to get new clothes. I'm already too fat. I just have to stop! Why can't I stop? I'm at risk for diabetes and heart attack and high blood pressure. I just have to stop!"

And the hand keeps bringing more food to my mouth.

Does that ring a bell? You want so desperately to stop but you can't. I did have all the reasons in the world to stop but I couldn't. The hand kept moving until there was nothing left.

Second example:

This one involves a goose skin.

I'm Jewish (but an agnostic, which I'll talk about when we get to Step Two), and one of our great celebration holidays is Chanukah, the Festival of Lights, which is held around Christmas-time. It could easily be called the Festival of Grease, because the food we traditionally ate on Chanukah was very greasy.

My mother had cooked a goose, as well as deep-fried pancakes over which we put the goose gravy. (Not that there really is goose gravy; it's just the fat of the goose that has dripped into the pan.) I don't remember the dessert we had, but I'm sure it was extremely rich. I was loaded to the gills after the meal—just packed. The ten or fifteen people who were at the dinner went into the living room, just around the corner from the kitchen.

I went to the kitchen to get a diet drink (I've always loved that!) and I saw the goose carcass on the cutting board with the goose skin hanging on the carcass. A goose is so fat that the skin just slips off.

Even though I was completely stuffed, I remember thinking to myself, "Well, I can't eat a lot, but I love the taste of goose skin, and we don't have it that often, so I'll just take a bite."

So I picked up the entire skin and took a small bite from it. It was still very hot from the oven. But the skin is very tough and I couldn't just take off a bit, so I put a bit more into my mouth to find a weak spot.

I blank out a bit here, but I remember suddenly realizing that I had the entire goose skin in my mouth and was chewing it frantically, because it was burning the inside of my mouth. Fat was spurting out between my lips. My cheeks were bulging. I kept on chewing until all the fat was gone from the skin, and then I swallowed the skin whole.

Third example:

This one involves a greasy spoon in Minneapolis, sometime in probably March 1962 or 1963. It was about 6 in the morning. I had just come off an overnight train ride and had a two-hour wait for a bus to go to my college south of Minneapolis. I started to wander down Hennepin Avenue, which was pretty grimy in those days.

I passed a greasy spoon that advertised a 39 cent breakfast with sausages and bacon, so I went in. It was packed with people who had clearly been up all night, hacking and coughing. I squeezed onto a stool at the counter and got my greasy meal and started to eat it.

Suddenly the man on my right vomited into his plate, and then fainted, and his head dropped right into the plate.

Here is the question which might separate a compulsive eater from a normal eater: What would a normal eater do and what did I do?

Yes, I turned my back on the man and continued to eat.

Summary:

It is perfectly obvious that I react very differently than normal eaters.

I can't stop once I've started. Normal eaters stop when they're full; normal eaters stop eating when something happens that's nauseating; even when normal eaters overeat, the next day they don't eat a lot. At one point or another they get unease or discomfort when they overeat, and their body basically tells them to stop.

I get that feeling with alcohol. I can't drink more than a glass and half of wine or beer (I don't like liquor) before I get this feeling of having had enough. I don't like that feeling, so I stop. Alcoholics don't feel that way when they drink. And I don't feel that way when I overeat.

The Big Book begins to define the alcoholic to whom it is addressed in Chapter Two, *There is a Solution*, on pages 20 to 24.

There the Big Book discusses the moderate and the hard drinkers, both of whom can give up alcohol if there is a good reason, and contrasts them with the *real* alcoholic. The real alcoholic is different. The real alcoholic can be either a moderate or a hard drinker, "but at some stage of his drinking career he begins to lose all control of his liquor consumption, once he starts to drink" (page 21). This is the allergy of the body—the lack of control once the substance is taken into the body—the phenomenon of craving.

Notice how different this is from the conventional and perhaps medical definition of an addict, where quantity–overindulgence–is the defining characteristic. The Big Book clearly says that quantity is not the defining characteristic. The defining characteristic, it says, is at the very least the inability to stop once the indulgence begins. Compulsive overeaters or alcoholics might be able to limit their number of binges or even the quantities they consume.

The real question is whether they get the phenomenon of craving once they start.

This explains why some diets and some diet programs work for others, but not for people like us. They are not compulsive eaters—at least the way the Big Book defines it. Diets "give back" binge foods in moderation after the weight is lost. Many people can eat those binge foods in moderation. But we can't–we get the phenomenon of craving.

There is another aspect That is the mental obsession, and the Big Book spends a lot of time discussing the mental obsession. But now that we've discussed the phenomenon of craving, it's time to abstain from those foods and eating behaviors that cause our craving.

Questions:

Here are some questions:

- What are my stories of overeating? Do I have the equivalent of a gallon of ice-cream, or a goose skin, a huge bag of potato chips, the whole container of cookies, or eating at times or in ways that normal people wouldn't eat?
- Have I experienced times when no matter how great my desire, I couldn't stop eating?
- Are there certain foods that once I start eating, I find it almost impossible to stop eating, until there's no more?
- Are there certain foods that I can't imagine ever giving up for good?
- Are there any patterns in my overeating? Are there certain times of the day, or certain kinds of situations, in which I find that I can't stop eating?

Step One, Part One—Developing a Plan of Eating:

In the last chapter I described the phenomenon of craving—what Dr. Silkworth describes in the Big Book as an "allergy" of the body. This is the first part of Step One.

Allergy doesn't mean a cough or a runny noise or a rash; it means simply an abnormal physical reaction to a physical substance. The allergy of the body we get when we overeat is the "phenomenon of craving". A phenomenon is an occurrence for which there is no explanation. We get cravings that we can't explain. But the essence of the cravings is that we simply cannot stop. Our body is telling us to eat, and we can't stop eating, just as we can't stop breathing or blinking our eyes—we may be able to suspend our breathing or blinking temporarily, but we simply can't stop.

The topic of this chapter comes from Dr. Silkworth in *The Doctor's Opinion.* He says: "Of course an alcoholic ought to be freed from his physical craving for liquor". *The Big Book takes sobriety for granted.*

No one attends AA thinking that he or she is going to continue drinking while working the steps. You stop drinking. You do *anything* to stop drinking, even if it means going to three or four meetings a day. And you work the steps.

What about us in OA? Is that OA's message—that we stop compulsive eating, do anything to stop eating compulsively (even if means going to as many meetings as we can, and phoning as many people as we can, and reading as much literature as we can), and work the steps? It should be.

We have to stop our craving, and the only way to stop the craving is to stop eating foods that cause our craving. (We also have to stop the eating behaviors that cause our cravings, and I discuss that below.) Our *Dignity of Choice* pamphlet makes that perfectly clear.

So how do we go about it? Sure, it's easier for an alcoholic to identify the substance that causes the allergy. For the alcoholic, it's alcohol in any form—whether in beer or wine or liquor or liqueur. But for the compulsive eater, *Dignity of Choice* says, and my experience confirms, that we can all differ in the kinds of substances that cause cravings for us.

For example, I can't eat butter in any form before I start craving it. But I know people in this program who can eat a pat or two of butter and don't get cravings. I can put some jam on my toast and don't get cravings, but I know people in this program who can't touch it at all.

In my discussions with other OAers from all over the world, I've come to the conclusion that, although there's an awful lot of overlap in our binge foods, in the rooms of OA there are people who can eat everything that I can't eat, and that I can eat everything that some people in OA can't eat at all. The *Dignity of Choice* makes this very clear—our plan of eating is an individual plan.

So how do we identify what causes our cravings? I can only tell you what I have done, and what people I've discussed this with have done. You have to figure it for yourself.

1. Abstain from individual binge foods.

I started by asking myself a simple question: What are the foods that I consistently overeat when I have the chance to eat them? What are the foods that I hunch over, hoarding, eating incessantly, blissing out?

The answers were clear for me: buttered popcorn, potato chips, shortbread, cheesecake, ice cream, deep-fried foods in general but in particular fried chicken (especially the skin), fatty meats (beef ribs and pork ribs and sausages and bacon), doughnuts—and many other similar kinds of foods.

Clearly any food that I couldn't stop eating when I started was a food that caused cravings. I had to eliminate those.

2. Abstain from individual binge ingredients.

But I went further than that. I asked myself whether there was a common ingredient in those foods, and if so, whether the presence of that common ingredient seemed to be a problem for me in general.

The answer was obvious—fat. I seemed to overeat almost anything that was high in fat content. It was usually fat mixed with salt or fat mixed with sugar. All fats had such a huge effect on me, but I realized as well that high-fat dairy products, like butter, were especially powerful for me.

Was sugar a problem for me? Well, I had eliminated most sugars from my eating—other than those with high fat content—years before I began to analyze my cravings. I just didn't eat foods that were sweet but not fat, like pop or some kinds of desserts. Very sweet foods actually gave me a headache. So I didn't include sugar in my list. Fat was clearly the culprit for me.

I therefore developed a plan of eating that eliminated foods with high fat content, and eliminated all high-fat dairy products in particular. I would not have a meal with a fat content higher than 10% of calories through fat. That meant I would have no deep-fried foods at all, and no snacks that contained a significant amount of fat (all potato chips, whether baked or not). I would examine content labels carefully for hidden fat content.

If given a choice between a food that had no fat and one that had even a little fat, I would choose the non-fat one (1% versus skim milk; spaghetti sauces with a little olive oil versus with no oil). I would trim all visible fats away from meat. I would not eat fatty meats. I would not eat any desserts and would have fruits instead.

I did that. It was hard work, but I did it. I also worked the steps, and just as promised at Step 9 in the Big Book, I was freed from my wish to eat all the foods that I had eliminated. I had recovered from compulsive eating! I could be around ice cream and not want it. That was a miracle. I was freed from the obsession. (I'll talk more about the obsession next chapter. It's the second part of Step One.)

But after a number of months I hadn't lost much weight. I was clearly taking in too much food, even though it was much healthier food than it was before.

I discussed this with my sponsor. I felt that Step Twelve required me to carry the message of recovery through the Twelve Steps. How could I carry that message if I wasn't at a healthy body weight? I felt I couldn't—I felt that I was missing something.

3. Abstain from individual binge eating behaviors.

Around this time I reread the OA Twelve and Twelve. On pages two and three the book mentions not simply binge foods but also "eating behaviors".

That got me thinking. I started to analyze my eating behaviors. Clearly I was eating more than my body needed, since I was still fat. What eating behaviors was I indulging in that caused me to eat too much of healthy foods?

I had a blinding flash of the obvious as I sat in my dentist's chair having my third or fourth or fifth crown put onto teeth that I had worn down or broken by chewing on bones and other things. My biggest eating behavior was simply chewing, keeping my mouth busy, constantly seeking oral gratification!

I realized that while I had adopted a plan of eating that eliminated high fats, I was constantly chewing. Where I used to chew buttered popcorn, I was now chewing carrots and celery and gum and hot-air popcorn. I was keeping my mouth busy—just as a popular weight-loss program used to tell me was necessary in order to keep from eating other foods.

What I discovered in my analysis was that my constant chewing kept my mouth wanting to chew more. At my mealtimes I was eating for the sake of chewing. Sure, it wasn't high fat foods, but it was food that contained calories of some sort. I was taking in too much food.

I remembered the time years before when I first joined OA and my plan of eating was so simple—three meals a day, nothing in between, a day at a time. I lost a lot of weight on that plan.

This was before I discovered the notion of the allergy of the body, so as soon as I lost that weight I took back a lot of foods I had eliminated, like ice cream and buttered popcorn and deep-fried foods, convinced at that time that my only problem was quantities. That is, of course, what almost all diets tell us. They tell us that once we lose the weight, we can eat everything—*so long* as we eat in moderation! But what's moderation to me once my allergy kicks in? It's impossible! Once I started eating ice cream, I couldn't stop!

One element of 3-0-1 clearly did work for me—and that was not eating between meals. That did something for me, I began to realize, that I wasn't doing this time. Eliminating any chewing or sucking between meals kept me from craving that oral gratification I used to get.

So I added another element to my plan of eating. In addition to eliminating all foods high in fat content, I stopped eating between meals.

This was difficult for me. I found myself chewing ice in my drinks, chewing or sucking on the ends of my pens, playing with my toothpick. But eventually I was able to stop chewing between meals entirely.

At the same time I also identified another eating behavior—this time a real blinding flash of the obvious: I liked to be stuffed to the gills! I wanted to be full all the time—not just pleasantly full, but stuffed. This had also led me to eating between meals, but in addition led to great quantities during my meals. Sure, I didn't want to eat ice cream, but I did want to be filled. So I would eat huge quantities of healthy foods, and they contained calories that kept my weight high.

So I added another element to my plan of eating. I would stop eating when I had eaten "enough". But how would I determine what was "enough"? It occurred to me that I could use my belly-button as a guide. I would stop eating when I felt as if the food had reached my belly-button, which was far better than when it reached almost up to the back of my mouth!

Those three elements—eliminating the fats, not eating or chewing or sucking between meals, stopping when I felt full up to my belly-button—constituted my new plan of eating, and as soon as I adopted that plan of eating, I lost my weight. That was about eleven years ago, and my weight has fluctuated but basically remained steady since I lost it.

I achieved a healthy body weight. How did I know? My doctor was happy. When I told some people I was a member of OA, they wondered why. And in OA people treated me as a person who had recovered. So I had every right to consider that my appearance was reasonable and healthy.

4. Continue to be honest and careful.

Over the past eleven years I've added more foods to my "don't eat" list. Although I kept to my plan of eating, I discovered that when I ate certain foods that were low in fat content I kept on eating them until they were all gone. This became true, for instance, for hot-air popcorn and for certain kinds of rice cakes; so I eliminated them. I discovered that high-fibre cereals that had sugar added made me more hungry; so I eliminated them.

Each time I did this it was easy, because I had already recovered and was working the steps to the best of my ability.

After 11 years of his being satisfied with my weight, in March 2005 my doctor told me that certain studies he had become aware of led him to think that I should be losing more weight.

So I did another analysis of my eating behaviors and of foods. Quantities were clearly the issue for me. I didn't think I was eating any particular foods that created problems. What could I do to eat less?

Well, instead of using my belly-button, I've been stopping eating when I begin to think about things other than food, such as when I begin to wonder whether I'm full. If I'm thinking about things other than food, my body has probably had enough. And I've discovered the amazing fact that twenty minutes after I stop eating, I'm really full! Go figure! So I lost ten pounds.

And when I went back to see my doctor in January 2007 he said he wanted me to lose more weight. So I looked at my eating again—but more importantly I also looked at my honesty by using Step 10. I left something on my plate and didn't go back for seconds. I also stopped looking at the scale, because that allowed me to relax. I lost another six pounds. My doctor was finally happy. I decided to continue on this journey, however, and as of the middle of 2007 I've lost another three or four pounds.

The lesson I take from this experience is that it's important always to be honest and vigilant, and not to relax in the program. It's easy to relax; we lose a lot of weight and feel better, and then we reach a plateau. It's important to be honest to see if that plateau is a reasonable plateau!

5. The individual's plan of eating.

I've had many many discussions with people all over the world about plans of eating that work for them. In all cases they've had to analyze their own eating behaviors and their own binge foods and binge ingredients. Some have had very few binge foods, but a number of bingeing eating behaviors, and others have had the reverse. Some have been unable to figure out what they can't eat, and prefer to figure out what they CAN eat. Some have been unable to find their belly-buttons or to find other ways to limit their intake, so they have counted calories or they have weighed and measured their foods (another way of counting calories, of course).

I've never thought these differences were a big deal. Each person finds his or her own way to find a plan of eating that works for him or her. There's no magic to it. We eliminate foods and eating behaviors that cause cravings and, if we need to lose weight, we find ways to limit our intake of food in general. Whether we do that in a "negative" way, as I do, by adopting a plan of eating that sets out what I CAN'T eat or do; or whether we do that in a "positive" way, as others do, by adopting a plan of eating that sets out what they CAN eat and how much of it and when they can, those are only methods of achieving the eliminating of foods and eating behaviors that cause cravings. All that is really needed is simple honesty.

When it comes to honesty, though, I think what's important is rigorous honesty. Some people jump very quickly to certain kinds of plans of eating because it seems to fit them, or because the plans are urged on them by other people in the program for whom the plans work, or maybe—just maybe!—because the plans allow them to hold onto certain foods which are really binge foods for them.

In all cases we must be rigorously honest. If, after having been abstinent for some time, you are still heavier than your body should be, then you owe it to yourself to examine your plan of eating. It may simply be a quantity issue. It may, however, really be that you are holding on to foods that are causing you cravings; and you're holding onto them because the plan of eating you chose for yourself (or someone else chose for you) didn't eliminate that food.

What I have noticed in OA is the prevalence of the "no sugar, no flour" plan of eating. I am certain that eliminating sugar and eliminating refined flour is quite healthy, but either of those two ingredients may not be the real issue. If doughnuts or ice-cream are foods that cause cravings, it might not be the sugar or the flour and sugar in them—it might be the fat in them, perhaps in combination with the sugar or the flour.

Questions:

Here are some questions:

- Have you developed a plan of eating that eliminates foods that cause you cravings?
- Have you developed a plan of eating that eliminates eating behaviors that cause you cravings?
- Are you holding on to foods that you secretly crave because you can't give them up?
- Have you adopted a plan of eating that works for you, or that works for someone else?
- Are there some foods that you keep eating in large quantities, even if they're allowed on your plan of eating? For instance, have you eliminated sugar and flour but still eat lots of high-fat foods
- If bread is a problem for you, for instance, is it really what you put on *top* of the bread—like butter or peanut butter or margarine or jam or honey—rather than the bread itself?
- In the end, if you have to lose weight, do you have a plan of eating that allows you to eat foods that have high amounts of non-nutritious calories? A little bit of fat, for instance, is necessary in our diet, but high amounts aren't. The sugars in fruits are part of a normal diet, but white sugar is of no value whatsoever. High-fiber grains are important to eat, but white flour is of very little value.

> This book is written from the perspective of compulsive overeating, but for those who compulsively restrict their eating (anorexics), or overeat but hide it by "purging" (bulimics), the same issues can hold true, if those eating behaviors have the same craving symptom.
>
> Just as with overeaters, not all anorexics and not all bulimics will identify with the "double whammy" described in the Big Book, but if they do, then the Twelve Steps of Overeaters Anonymous can provide a solution.
>
> Developing a Plan of Eating would require both a food analysis and an eating behavior analysis, of course. Of course one would abstain from the compulsive eating behaviors, like restricting or like purging. It would be valuable, however, to see if some foods or food ingredients or mixtures of ingredients caused cravings as well. Those who binge and purge are not different at all from those who binge, other than finding ways of hiding the symptoms. Those who restrict might be restricting because they have binged, and it would be worthwhile to see whether or not the binging was usually over particular foods or ingredients, rather than over "everything".

Step One, Part Two—the Obsession of the Mind:

In the last chapter I discussed the first part of Step One from the Big Book perspective—the allergy of the body (the phenomenon of craving) we get when we eat certain foods or indulge in certain eating behaviors. In that chapter I especially emphasized what the Big Book takes for granted—that we find a plan of eating that eliminates those foods and/or eating behaviors which cause our cravings—that we become, in a word, abstinent.

Now it's time to talk about the second part of Step One—the obsession of the mind.

As the Big Book points out, this mental obsession is our real problem.

If our only problem were that we get physical cravings that overwhelm us, there would be a simple solution, when you think about it: just don't eat those foods or indulge in those eating behaviors; everything would be fine. In effect, that's what we did when we went on diets.

Consider this: right now, I eat shrimp and enjoy it. But if I developed an allergy to shrimp, as many people have, and I would suffer a tremendous shock to my system that could kill me, I think I would look at shrimp as a poison. I would avoid it like the plague. I would say to myself, "Well I used to like it, but I sure don't like it now. Why would I eat anything that killed me?"

Yet before OA I ate all kinds of food that I knew perfectly well were killing me!

Our real problem, as the Big Book points out, is that we keep finding excuses to go back to those foods and those eating behaviors:

> Why does he behave like this? If hundreds of experiences have shown him that one drink means another debacle with all its attendant suffering and humiliation, why is it he takes that one drink? Why can't he stay on the water wagon? What has become of the common sense and will power that he still sometimes displays with respect to other matters?
>
> Perhaps there never will be a full answer to these questions. Opinions vary considerably as to why the alcoholic reacts differently from normal people. We are not sure why, once a certain point is reached, little can be done for him. We cannot answer the riddle.
>
> We know that while the alcoholic keeps away from drink, as he may do for months or years, he reacts much like other men. We are equally positive that once he takes any alcohol whatever into his system, something happens, both in the bodily and mental sense, which makes it virtually impossible for him to stop. The experience of any alcoholic will abundantly confirm this.
>
> These observations would be academic and pointless if our friend never took the first drink, thereby setting the terrible cycle in motion. Therefore, the main problem of the alcoholic centers in his mind, rather than in his body. (pages 22-3 of the Big Book)

Why do we keep going back? What gets us to eat the first bite?

Well, one thing that's obvious is that virtually every diet and every book on losing weight, and many many doctors and dietitians and nutritionists whom we consult, all seem to say that once we have lost our weight we *can* go back to eating ALL the foods we used to eat, but *this* time in *moderation*! It's just a matter of will power, or maybe they phrase it as won't power. They can't imagine why we would eat in large quantities again.

What is their problem? They don't understand that we have a physical problem. They don't understand that, unlike the normal eater, we don't get unease or discomfort when we overeat—rather, we crave more. They simply don't understand our allergy of the body.

So, on the advice of our doctors, or other health-care professionals, the diets in magazines and books, and the weight-loss programs, we lose our weight and then take back our weekly scoop of ice cream, or two cookies, or comfort food. And then the weekly scoop becomes bigger, and then becomes more frequent, and then becomes the hand going to the mouth and we're asking ourselves why we can't stop.

But wait, as the infomercials say, there's more!

Here's my list. I bet you can add to it!

I deserve this because:

- I'm so depressed. What will make me feel better?
- I'm so happy! How can I celebrate?
- I've been very good for a year. A month. A week. An hour.
- I didn't eat the bun . . . the last french fry . . . the second helping.
- I worked so hard making it.
- I feel guilty because I didn't work so hard making it.

I need this because:

- No one loves me.
- How will I fit in otherwise?
- Too many people love me.
- I want to die and overeating will kill me. But it's a nice way to commit suicide. My spouse will not feel guilty when I die.
- Nothing else will remove the hurt, if only for a second.

I must have this because:

- They made it especially for me. How can I refuse?
- It's free!
- I'll never be able to have this food again.
- It will go to waste.
- Everyone is looking at me; how can I refuse?

I can have this because:

- I'm standing up. It doesn't count!
- It's a stone ground whole-grain cinnamon bun made with organic molasses and cold-pressed organic oil! So it's really good for me and doesn't count!
- She's not looking, so it doesn't count.
- I have to taste it in order to see whether it's okay.
- At least people can see what my weakness is.

Ring some bells?

So what are these curious excuses?

Mental, not simply emotional

The Big Book describes them as a mental obsession, not simply an emotional one. Certainly some of these are emotional excuses. But some of them are just plain stupid ones.

We often hear in OA that our problem is physical, emotional, and spiritual. The Big Book doesn't use the word "emotional" to describe our problem. It uses the word "mental". That's because our reasons for returning to the food are often just insane, and sometimes don't depend on how we're feeling at all.

We could have had a normal day, have lost a lot of weight by eliminating ice cream from our diet, and be in a supermarket where they're offering a sample of new flavor of ice cream, and find ourselves eating that sample before we even know what we're doing.

It doesn't do us any good to figure out what was eating us. What does us good is to realize that we keep finding excuses to go back to foods that we know, deep in our hearts, we can't eat without developing cravings.

This is the real problem, as the Big Book points out. There is no answer. "We cannot answer the riddle." We just know that we do it.

The whole of the chapter *More About Alcoholism* (beginning on page 30) describes the mental obsession. It is the same obsession whatever we're addicted to—whether gambling or alcohol or cocaine or food or emotions. It is that excuse we give to ourselves for going back.

> It is not surprising that our drinking careers have been characterized by countless vain attempts to prove we could drink like other people. The idea that somehow, someday he will control and enjoy his drinking is the great obsession of every abnormal drinker. The persistence of this illusion is aston-

> ishing. Many pursue it into the gates of insanity or death. (Page 30)

In that chapter the Big Book describes four addicts who return to their addiction. One of them has not had a drink for 25 years, and thinks that a long period of sobriety enables him to drink like normal people. One of them has a bad day, and persuades himself that whiskey won't hurt him if taken with milk. One of them keeps going back to jaywalking even though he has suffered tremendous physical damage, and can't explain himself at all. And one of them has a great day, and finds himself thinking that it would be nice to have cocktails with his dinner.

> There was always the curious mental phenomenon that parallel with our sound reasoning there inevitably ran some insanely trivial excuse for taking the first drink. Our sound reasoning failed to hold us in check. The insane idea won out. Next day we would ask ourselves, in all earnestness and sincerity, how it could have happened.
>
> In some circumstances we have gone out deliberately to get drunk, feeling ourselves justified by nervousness, anger, worry, depression, jealousy or the like. But even in this type of beginning we are obliged to admit that our justification for a spree was insanely insufficient in the light of what always happened. We now see that when we began to drink deliberately, instead of casually, there was little serious or effective thought during the period of premeditation of what the terrific [horrible] consequences might be. (Page 37)

Yes, says the Big Book, sometimes we have felt justified by extreme emotions. But we've also had trivial excuses.

That fits my experience well. I can be on a diet and have thoughts like, "That looks good, but I can't eat it. I won't eat it. It's not good for me. I'm doing so well on my diet." But I'll simultaneously have other thoughts like, "It's only a bit, you've never had that taste before, you can have just one." And then the second thought just overpowers the first, and I'm back again. I've become a yo-yo dieter.

The Mental Obsession:

The Big Book's characterization of this is as a mental obsession. An obsession is a thought that overpowers all other thought. It is an obsession over which we have no mental defence. We can't stop ourselves from thinking. You try it. I'll pay you $5,000.00 if you don't think of the word "rhinoceros" for 20 seconds! Did you win the bet? I doubt it. We can't control our thinking. And we can't control the mental obsession.

We have two lines of thought running parallel to each other, just like the proverbial good and bad angels perched on our two shoulders. The "good" thought is, "I can't eat this stuff, it'll make me fat, I won't eat it, I want to be thin." The "bad" thought is, "Ah, come on. It's okay, because . . . [fill in the rationalization!]." Then suddenly a click occurs, and the bad thought just overpowers the good thought, and we begin again.

The Double Whammy:

The *first part* of our addiction is that we are powerless over food—we get uncontrollable physical cravings when we eat certain foods or indulge in certain eating behaviors. This is the **allergy of the body**.

The *second part* is that we can't manage our lives in relation to our powerlessness over food—we get mental obsessions that send us back to those foods and those eating behaviors that we know will cause us the uncontrollable cravings. This is the **obsession of the mind**.

We have what Dr. Silkworth called the "double whammy". We can't stop once we've started; and we can't stop from starting again. We're doomed.

That is Step One—the realization that we are doomed. And we're not doomed because of our allergy of the body, but because of our mental obsession. And we begin to realize that the only solution that will ever work with us is something that gets rid of our mental obsession. And we know we can't do it by ourselves, because we can't stop the thinking that keeps sending us back.

Note that Step One as written on the wall is *not* "We admitted that we were powerless over food AND that our life had become unmanageable." It's "We admitted that we were powerless over food—that our lives had become unmanageable."

That means that we have to admit that our life had become unmanageable *in relation to our powerlessness over food.* If someone had tried to convince me when I joined the program that my whole life was unmanageable, I would have left the program. My life was fine (or apparently fine) except for the food. But Step One doesn't require us to accept anything but our powerlessness over food!

Maybe now we will be ready for Step Two. If Step One is the problem of powerlessness, then Step Two is the solution of power!

William D. Silkworth, M.D.

Questions:

Here are questions for you:

- What excuses have you used to go back to compulsive eating?
- Have any of your reasons for going back to compulsive eating ever ever ever turned out to be reasonable?
- Have you ever gone back to compulsive eating before you even realized you were doing it?
- Does your experience show that you have been capable, on your own, of ultimately resisting an excuse to go back to compulsive eating?
- Does your experience show that you have returned to compulsive eating only because you've felt emotionally justified, or have you had trivial excuses as well?

Are you now convinced that in yourself there is no solution to the double whammy? This is crucial. Do you still think there's a chance? Or do you know that you are doomed?

CHARLES B. TOWNS HOSPITAL

293 Central Park West New York, New York

For ALCOHOLISM and DRUG ADDICTION

ANY PHYSICIAN having an addict problem is invited to write for Hospital literature.

This institution has specialized in addictions for over 30 years. Its method of treatment has been fully described in THE JOURNAL A. M. A.; in The Handbook of Therapy, from the A. M. A. Press; and in other scientific literature. The treatment is a regular hospital procedure, and provides a definite means for eliminating the toxic products of alcohol and drugs from the tissues. A complete Department of Physical Therapy, with gymnasium and other facilities for physical rebuilding, is maintained. Operated as an "open" institution. Physicians are not only invited but urged to accompany and stay with their patients.

Located Directly Across from Central Park

Step Two:

In Step One we found complete despair—powerlessness. We cannot solve the problem of our compulsive eating by ourselves. In Step Two we will find hope—power. A power greater than ourselves *will* restore us to sanity.

Step One is the problem. Step Two is the solution.

The Big Book discusses Step Two in part of "Bill's Story" and in the whole of "We Agnostics".

Most of the discussion of Step Two in the Big Book is aimed at persons who do not believe in a personal god—agnostics (who have come to the conclusion that they will never know whether there is a God or not) or atheists (who believe there is no God). Therefore most of today's share will concentrate on reasons why a person who does not believe in God would want to find a Higher Power through the Twelve Steps.

Why, then, would a person who believes in a specific God be interested in this discussion? There are two reasons.

1 The religious person will someday in sponsoring meet someone like me, and he or she should know the arguments to help someone like me.

2 There is an extremely important page of the Big Book which the person who believes in God but who is still suffering from compulsive eating ought to understand—if he or she is to recover!

In the following discussion, I take for granted that we have accepted our powerlessness over food—that Step One for us is a reality. (Note that we don't "take" Step One. There is no concept in the Big Book that we "take" it or "do" it. It is rather that we *acknowledge* our powerlessness, we *accept* our powerlessness.)

We understand the "double whammy" of not being able to stop when we start (the physical allergy), and of not being able to stop from starting again (the mental obsession), and realize that there is no hope for us on our own.

Because we have this mental obsession, we are insane. We need to have constant sanity to be able to say, "I don't want to eat foods or indulge in eating behaviors that cause me uncontrollable cravings."

Those who have read "Bill's Story" will recall that in his worst moment of despair—after Dr. Silkworth tells him about the double whammy and he experiences the truth of it and the hopelessness of his situation—he was visited by his friend Ebby, who was sober; and that when Bill asked him how he had become sober, Ebby told him that he had found religion. This hit Bill hard. He was an agnostic. He could not believe in the God of religion, something he had rejected for many years.

What was Bill to do? He saw in his friend a real miracle:

> Like myself, he had admitted complete defeat. Then he had, in effect, been raised from the dead, suddenly taken from the scrap heap to a level of life better than the best he had ever known! Had this power originated in him? Obviously it had not. There had been no more power in him than there was in me at the minute; and this was none at all. Never mind the musty past; here sat a miracle directly across the kitchen table. He shouted great tidings. (pages 11 and 12)

Here is the point at which we see the value that all of our past experience is able to bring to the compulsive eater who still suffers. If it is clear that we used to be like the person who still suffers, but are now different as a result of the Twelve Steps, then we fill the prospect with both *despair* (Step One—s/he can't do it on his/her own) and *hope* (Step Two—it can be done!).

But how could Bill have that miracle if he did not believe in God?

Ebby then gave Bill, and AA, and OA and all other Twelve Step programs, a great gift. Although he was part of an evangelical Christian movement (the Oxford Groups), he didn't try to persuade Bill to believe in any kind of God. He said, "Why don't you choose your own conception of God?" (page 12)

That was enough for Bill to work on. "It was only a matter of being willing to believe in a Power greater than myself. Nothing more was required of me to make my beginning."

This theme is expanded in the chapter "We Agnostics". It is designed to give the still-suffering alcoholic reasons to be willing. It is NOT designed to prove the existence of God. I misread it for years. I thought it was designed to prove the existence of God, and of course it fails in that respect.

Outline of *We Agnostics*:

The chapter is divided into three major sections.

The *first section*, from page 44 to page 48, poses the essential dilemma facing a person who does not believe in God.

The *second section*, from page 48 to page 54, presents three powerful arguments on why one should be willing to find a Higher Power.

The *third section*, from page 54 to page 55, gives the reality of fundamental belief and is the section of extreme importance to the believer as well as to the non-believer. (There is also a fourth anecdotal section from page 55 to page 57 providing experiential testimony.) I'll summarize each section.

First section–the dilemma:

Pages 44 - 48: Because we cannot recover on our own, we are doomed unless we find a Power greater than ourselves. This book is all about finding that Higher Power. But that's a real problem for people who don't believe in God. About half of us were like that. Don't be prejudiced by the words we use in this book to describe a Higher Power. It's your own conception that's important. And don't worry. You don't HAVE to believe in a Higher Power in order to work the Steps. You only have to be WILLING to believe.

Second section–the reasons:

Pages 48 - 54. Here are the three reasons the agnostic or atheist should be willing to try what this book offers.

First reason (pages 48 to the top of 51): *Scientifically speaking, a theory that's grounded in fact—that works—is worth trying out.* All of us believe in theories about electricity even though we've never seen the atoms upon which that theory is based; but the theories work for us, and therefore we believe them. Our theory is that a Higher Power can restore us to sanity. Clearly that theory works. Therefore the agnostic or atheist should try it!

Second reason (pages 51 to the bottom of 53): *No real progress is ever made in this world unless we challenge established ideas that don't work and become willing to try new ideas that might work.* Until someone was willing to try out the idea that the earth was round or that the earth circled the sun, little progress was made in navigation; until someone was willing to try out the idea that a heavier-than-air flying machine could be built, it was not built. The idea of the agnostic or atheist that he or she can handle his or her own addiction doesn't work. Our idea that we need a Higher Power does work. Therefore the agnostic or atheist should try it!

Third reason (pages 53 to the bottom of 54): *Regardless of the protestations of the atheist or agnostic, he or she DOES believe in things that are in fact more powerful than he or she is.* The atheist or agnostic believes in his or her own reasoning; actually worships things—like love or money—that can't be justified using logic. As a matter of fact, the things the atheist

The Appendix on *Spiritual Experience* was placed into the second printing of the Big Book, in 1941. It was put there to make it clear that a sudden spiritual epiphany was not the norm for AAers when they did the steps. What *was* usual was a gradual spiritual awakening. So Bill Wilson made certain that when it came time to reprint the Big Book, after the first 5,000 copies had been distributed, the Big Book would contain that explanation. The Appendix is important for three other reasons.

First, it provides a completely non-religious and in a real sense a non-spiritual definition of spiritual experience or spiritual awakening—a "personality change sufficient to bring about recovery from alcoholism", and later on, "a profound alteration in his reaction to life".

This opens up the program for people who have no sense of a God at all. If I have received a personality change that has been sufficient to overcome my compulsive overeating, then I have had a spiritual awakening. I don't have to argue with anybody at all about whether or not I've accepted "God" in my life.

Second, it talks about achieving recovery "in a few months", which should give a real ray of hope.

Third, it contains that wonderful quote (wrongly) attributed to Herbert Spencer: "There is a principle which is a bar against all information, which is proof against all arguments and which cannot fail to keep a man in everlasting ignorance—that principle is contempt prior to investigation."

It appears that Herbert Spencer didn't say this. It was written by a minister named William Paley. See the fascinating lengthy article by Michael StGeorge currently (2017) available at **http://anonpress.org/spencer/ or** www.aabibliography.com/pdffiles/Survival_of_a_Fitting_Quotation.pdf.

or the agnostic worships are what give him or her the essence of his or her life. "It was impossible to say we had no capacity for faith, or love, or worship. In one form or another we had been living by faith and little else" (page 54). So the atheist or the agnostic DOES believe in something that he or she can't touch or see and can't prove. So why not TRY the idea that this program will give you a sense of a higher power? It can't hurt!

Chapter Two, *There is a Solution*, contains a summary of the issues relating to the allergy of the body and the obsession of the mind. It is well worth reading!

It also contains the wonderful story at pages 26 through 28 of "a certain American businessman" (Rowland Hazard), who had consulted with the great psychoanalyst Dr. Carl Jung for some time, yet who went back to alcoholism as soon as he left. Dr. Jung told him his condition was hopeless unless he could find a spiritual experience; but simply being religious wasn't enough.

Rowland found the Oxford Groups, which used a few simple actions to gain a spiritual experience. As one of them put it, you get honest with yourself (Step Four), you get honest with another human being (Step Five), you make up for what you've done wrong (Step Nine), you trust in God (Step Eleven), and you help others (Step Twelve). He had a spiritual experience and stopped drinking. He brought his message to Ebby Thacher, who then brought it to Bill Wilson. Bill adapted those steps to create the Twelve Steps.

Just before Dr. Jung died, Bill wrote him a lengthy letter thanking him for the role he played in developing AA. Dr. Jung wrote a brilliant letter back. Both of those letters can be found in the great AA publication, *The Language of the Heart*—a collection of Bill's writings in the AA *Grapevine*. Dr. Jung's concept was that alcoholism is the low-level thirst for spirituality—equal to our OA low-level hunger for spirituality—and that what AA (and OA) provides is real spirituality through the support of a like-minded community and actions which bring us closer to our spiritual center.

Some doubt has been placed on the accuracy of the Big Book's account of Rowland's contact with Dr. Jung, although the spiritual basis and the ideas behind it have not been questioned;

See **www.wejoy.org/pdf/Rowland%20Hazard.pdf** for a attempt to figure out when Rowland consulted with Dr. Jung and what really influenced Rowland to pursue the Oxford Groups.

Third section–deep down within us is our fundamental conception of a Higher Power:

Pages 54 - 55: *Faith is part of our makeup, and in that is the fundamental idea of God.*

> Actually we were fooling ourselves, for deep down in every man, woman, and child, is the fundamental idea of God. It may be obscured by calamity, by pomp, by worship of other things, but in some form or other it is there. We finally saw that faith in some kind of God was a part of our make-up, just as much as the feeling we have for a friend. Sometimes we had to search fearlessly, but He was there. He was as much a fact as we were. We found the Great Reality deep down within us. In the last analysis it is only there that He may be found. It was so with us. (page 55)

So ultimately we will find a Higher Power "deep down within us".

But—*and this is what is so important EVEN for the person who believes in God*—that Higher Power is "obscured by calamity, pomp, by worship of other things" (page 55). Put in other words, our Higher Power is blocked by bad things that have happened to us, by a sense of self-importance, and by worship of other things.

The Steps unblock us from our Higher Power:

Here is the essence of what the Twelve Steps do for us! The Steps REMOVE the things that BLOCK us from the Higher Power deep down within us!

As soon as the block is removed, we have contact with that Higher Power. And as soon as we have contact with that Higher Power, we become sane. And becoming sane means that we no longer want to return to the foods and eating behaviors that create uncontrollable cravings. We will see in the discussion of Step Four that the Big Book talks about being "blocked" (page 71) from the "sunlight of the spirit" (page 66).

So whether we believe in God or don't believe in God, if we are not sane when it comes to food, it is clear that we have blocked off our route to sanity. The only solution we know is to get rid of the blocks. To do that we work the Twelve Steps.

What to say to the person who doesn't believe in God:

The question to ask, therefore, of people who don't believe in God is what concepts or ideas or feelings they DO believe in that are more important than they are: What gives them any meaning at all in their lives?

Any person desperate enough to come to OA and who is relatively honest will be able to answer that question at least in part. That person will usually come up with LOVE at the very least—"Who of us had not loved something or somebody?" (page 54) They may come up with high ideals, as I did when asked that question, like Truth, or Justice, or Beauty. Or they may come up with Doing Good, Being Useful; or Not Doing Harm, Being Part of the World; or simply Intuitively Doing the Right Thing, Being Serene. Which of us can't come up with a list of one or two or three things that motivate us, things that we may have trouble attaining, but that we wish we could attain?

If we use the Big Book's image of blocking the Higher Power which is "deep down within us", we can see that our fundamental idea of a Higher Power is really the concepts or the ideals which give us whatever motivation in life we have. Some people, religious people, call that God, and give it a personality and various attributes. Some people don't. For the purposes of the Twelve Steps, it really makes no difference.

A Higher Power gives us direction.

A *personal* God gives us direction by telling us what to do, perhaps through our holy scriptures or through a revelation or through meditation or through "signs"—things that happens to us that have meaning for us. That God, in effect, "pushes" us from behind to go to a particular direction.

A Higher Power consisting of *values* gives us direction by being a beacon, a North Pole, a compass point—a place to go towards. That God, in effect, "pulls" us in a particular direction.

The image that makes sense to me is that of a compass. Out of the 360 degrees on the compass, there is the one degree direction of Truth, Love, Justice, and Beauty. The other 359 degrees consist of *my* way; and not one of those paths has ever worked!

What to say to the person who does believe in God:

The question to ask of those who do believe in God is, "Do you accept that something is blocking you off from your God?" Most people asked that question will answer Yes. They will talk about their religious schooling or upbringing that caused them not to love their God but to fear Him. They will talk about the scars of their lives and think that their God has punished them. Or they will simply acknowledge that their religious activity has become mechanical and not meaningful to them. They will intuitively understand the notion of being blocked from God.

One religious person I spoke to talked about being "functionally agnostic" before he worked the steps—although he believed in God, he didn't act according to his beliefs. That made sense to me.

For those who have rejected their childhood religion because of various issues, there is also the wonderful and calming option of their being able to choose the "best part" of their God—by focusing on the love and the understanding and the compassion that is at the very least PART of their religious upbringing without having to embrace the WHOLE of the god of their religion.

The Steps provide us with a Higher Power:

What the Big Book actually promises is that working the Twelve Steps *will* remove the blocks that keep us from our Higher Power, however we have conceived It, and that Higher Power will enter into our lives and give us sanity. There's no promise that we will believe in the God of a religion at all. The only promise is that we will have sanity—that we will feel a strength and power that we know did not exist in us when we were trying to deal with our problems on our own.

The Appendix on *Spiritual Experience* makes that very clear. A spiritual experience, the Appendix says, can

> Step Two is not a huge step to take the Big Book way. As a matter of fact, we don't *take* Step Two at all.
>
> It is simply a sense of what a Higher Power could be, and a willingness to work the steps of the program in order to see if such a Higher Power can be found.
>
> Aside from setting out a number 2 step on page 59, the Big Book never mentions Step Two as a step. There is simply the discussion of being open to finding a higher power as set out in three chapters in the Big Book—*Bill's Story*, *There is a Solution*, and *We Agnostics*.

be slow, an awakening, and not sudden. And it is characterized by "a personality change sufficient to overcome alcoholism".

Step Two only requires that we be willing to try to find our Higher Power. That's all. Our willingness is enough to start the process of working the Twelve Steps. When we work the Twelve Steps, we find that automatically (guaranteed by end of Step Nine!) we become sane in relation to food, without any effort on our part in dealing with food (see the Hidden Promises at the bottom of page 84 and top of page 85)!

For agnostics and atheists, I can only say this as personal testimony. I began this program manyh many years ago as an agnostic. I am still an agnostic, a very skeptical agnostic. But I have recovered in this program, a day at a time: I am sane about foods and eating behaviors that cause me uncontrollable craving. Therefore I have achieved a spiritual awakening as promised by the Steps, and I will continue to have that spiritual awakening so long as I continue to work the Steps and maintain a fit spiritual condition.

So to all of you who are atheists and agnostics, don't despair at all! Just do the steps! The Big Book guarantees that if you do the steps, by the end of Step Nine you will have a personality change sufficient to overcome compulsive eating—and in the words of the Big Book, that IS a spiritual awakening! Certainly, if you're like me, it will be a miracle!

And for believers, my experience with countless other believers in OA is that the Steps remove the blockage between them and their God, and those believers end up affirming their faith in deep and ultimately mystical ways.

What Step Two is and what it is not:

If we are powerless as individuals, can we derive hope from those in OA, or those in other 12-step programs, who have clearly recovered from their addictions?

There appears to be an interpretation of OA's Twelve and Twelve which gives the impression that Step Three is a step we can't take until we're really really really ready, and that if we don't suddenly find ourselves actually turning our will and our life over to the care of our god, we haven't completed Step Three. From a Big Book point of view, that doesn't appear to be the case at all. Step Three is simply a decision to go on with the steps. The Big Book promises that we will have our will and our life turned over to the care of our god by Step Nine.

That's the only real question. If we can feel some hope that people who are just like us have recovered by working the Twelve Steps, then maybe, just maybe, we can try it ourselves. Step Two is only hope – nothing more. It is the promise of what happens IF we work the Twelve Steps. It doesn't give us a Higher Power and doesn't require us to adopt one.

Questions:

So, some questions:

- Do you accept that on your own you are powerless over those foods and eating behaviors that cause you uncontrollable cravings?
- Is what you're doing about your powerlessness working?
- Do you accept that there are those people who have been as powerless as you who are full of a power that has overcome their powerlessness?
- Are you willing to do what those people say gave them power?
- If you don't believe in God, is there anything you believe in that is more important than you are? If so, what? Call that God.
- If you believe in God, do you feel cut off —blocked—from God?
- Are you ready to go forward?

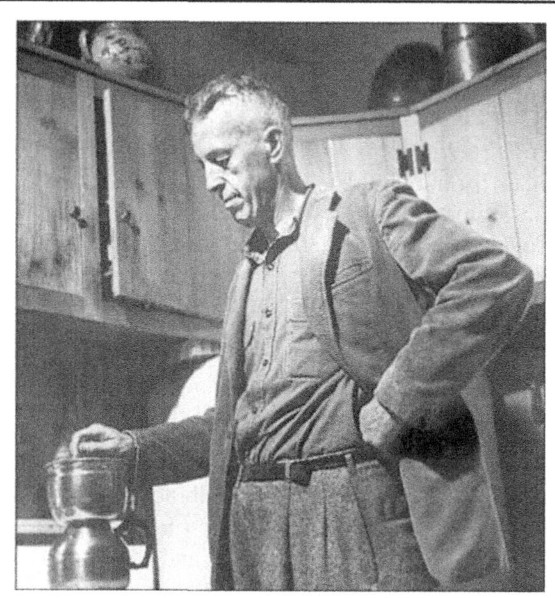

AA WORLD SERVICES, INC.

SOBER: Bill Wilson in his kitchen, 1952

Step Three:

Step Three is discussed in the Big Book from the bottom of page 60 to the bottom of page 63. We will find that this section contains extremely important information, but that the step itself is a relatively simple step. It is the first step in which we actually DO something, but what we do is not that complicated or time-consuming.

Before we start discussing Step Three, however, it's important to discuss the first two and half pages of Chapter Five ("How It Works")—pages 58 to 60.

Page 58 stresses "rigorous honesty". It points out that the only thing that stands in the way of recovery is a lack of the ability to be honest with one's self. It also asks us if we are committed "to go to any lengths" to find recovery.

Page 59 to the top of page 60 sets out the Twelve Steps of Alcoholics Anonymous, which have been adapted for OA, with only two changes (in Steps One—what we're powerless over—and Twelve—to whom we try to carry the message).

The original steps:

Originally AA had six steps and not twelve. There are many sources for this statement (see *AA Comes of Age* and *The Language of the Heart*, both available from AA); you can find one source in the Big Book on page 292 of the third edition or page 263 of the fourth edition.

As you may know, the Big Book was written as a do-it-yourself manual for people who were not able to have contact with AA members who had recovered.

Bill Wilson, who basically wrote the Big Book, considered it necessary to make certain that he provided more detail for the steps than existed previously. He therefore added what turned out to be six more steps.

That's important to know because the six steps that he added are clearly not steps which have the same kind of significance as the original six steps.

Here are the twelve steps of Overeaters Anonymous. Immediately after six of them, in [brackets], I've put the original six steps (as found first in the Big Book on the pages above, underlined, and then in *italics* from *AA Comes of Age* on page 160):

1. **We admitted we were powerless over food, that our lives had become unmanageable.**

   [Complete deflation. *We admitted that we were licked, that we were powerless over alcohol.*]

2. **Came to believe that a Power greater than ourselves could restore us to sanity.**

3. **Made a decision to turn our will and our lives over to the care of God *as we understood Him*.**

4. **Made a searching and fearless moral inventory of ourselves.**

   [Moral inventory. *We made a moral inventory of our defects or sins.*]

5. **Admitted to God, to ourselves, and to another human being the exact nature of our wrongs.**

   [Confession. *We confessed or shared our shortcomings with another person in confidence.*]

6. **Were entirely ready to have God remove all these defects of character.**

7. **Humbly asked Him to remove our shortcomings.**

8. **Made a list of all persons we had harmed, and became willing to make amends to them all.**

9. **Made direct amends to such people wherever possible, except when to do so would injure them or others.**

   [Restitution. *We made restitution to all those we had harmed by our drinking.*]

10. **Continued to take personal inventory and when were wrong promptly admitted it.**

11. **Sought through prayer and meditation to improve our conscious contact with God *as we understood Him*, praying only for knowledge of His will for us and the power to carry that out.**

    [Dependence and guidance from a Higher Power. *We prayed to whatever God we thought there was for power to practice these precepts.*]

12. **Having had a spiritual awakening as the result of these steps, we tried to carry this**

message to compulsive overeaters, and to practice these principles in all our affairs.

[Continued work with other alcoholics. *We tried to help other alcoholics, with no thought of reward in money or prestige*.]

So you can see that the original six steps were basically Steps One, Four, Five, Nine, Eleven, and Twelve. The other steps were added in order to make certain that there were no loopholes. They were not and are still not the essence of the program. We'll see how this plays out as we go.

Step Three is merely a *decision* to do the rest of the steps:

Step Three is therefore not a huge step that requires lots of time and action. It is simply an acknowledgement of the *consequences* of the willingness through hope that we developed in Step Two.

If you are willing to try to find a Higher Power through the steps (Step Two), then you have to make a decision to *work* the steps. And that really is all Step Three is—a *decision*.

I could decide to write an article on Step Three, but if I don't actually sit down at my computer and write it, my decision to write is of no value whatsoever.

So my decision to turn my will and my life over to the care of my Higher Power is *simply a decision.* It's not actually turning my will and my life over. It's just a *decision* to do that. In order to turn my will and my life over, I have to get rid of the things in myself that are blocking me from my Higher Power. We'll see the complete truth of this statement when we discuss Step Four next chapter.

The discussion preceding Step Three:

So what of the discussion on pages 60 through 64 about Step Three? Why is it there?

I believe there are two main purposes of that discussion. The first is to explain WHY we have to make the decision to turn our will and our life over; this involves a discussion of "selfishness" from the Big Book perspective. The second is to tell us WHAT we have to do in order to make that decision; this involves setting out the words of the Step Three prayer.

The pages discussing the WHY are divided into two parts. The first part (bottom of page 60 through bottom of page 63) discusses the WILL part of "turn our will and our lives over to the care of" our Higher Power. The second part (bottom of page 63 to top of page 64) discusses the LIFE part of "turning our willing and our life over".

The Big Book discusses what it considers the universal characteristic of the alcoholic/compulsive eater. It uses as an example the actor in a play who wants to be the director/producer of the play, who knows the play would go much better if his or her way were adopted.

I remember where I was sitting (in a small basement restaurant) when my first sponsor pointed those words out. They struck me right to the heart. Of course I wanted to be in charge! And it was the fact that I wasn't in charge, that the play wasn't going my way, that was at the heart of my problems!

The Big Book uses a number of words to describe that universal characteristic: self-willed, self-propulsion, self-seeker, manager, self-centered, egocentric, selfish, self-centered, fearful, self-deluding, self-pitying.

These words are all used to describe a person who basically wants life to go his or her way, *regardless of the motivation*.

So from the perspective of the Big Book, the motivation of wanting life to go your way is irrelevant.

Sometimes the motives can be quite outer-directed. Certainly I have my own convictions of how the world could be a better place and people could get along better, and my motives are really quite good in that respect. I don't suffer from the effects of poverty or torture or suppression or imminent disease or death; yet I would like to have a world in which other people don't suffer from that either. My children are adults now, and I want them to be happy in their lives purely because I love them.

Sometimes, however, the motives can be quite inner-directed—or selfish in the dictionary definition. I want people to like me so I can feel good about myself; I want people to give me business to keep me financially secure; I wanted girlfriends (I'm happily married now!) to satisfy physical and social desires; when my kids were young, I didn't want them to embarrass me by bad behavior.

And sometimes there's a mix of motives. I don't want close relatives to get very sick both because I don't want them to suffer AND because I don't want the inconvenience of having to take care of them. I don't want there to be bombs both because I don't want innocent people to suffer AND because I don't want to die.

But whatever the motives, I want life to go my way rather than the way it is going. I therefore understand wanting to be the director of the play rather than the actor. It makes a lot of sense to me. Sometimes I tried to impose my will on others. Sometimes I just gave up and played the martyr. But in all cases I KNEW the right way – and it wasn't happening. And that was killing me!

The Big Book's special definition of *selfish*:

The Big Book says at page 62:

> Selfishness - self-centeredness! That, we think, is the root of our troubles. Driven by a hundred forms of fear, self-delusion, self-seeking, and self-pity, we step on the toes of our fellows and they retaliate. So our troubles, we think, are basically of our own making. They arise out of ourselves, and the alcoholic is an extreme example of self-will run riot, though he usually doesn't think so. Above everything, we alcoholics must be rid of this selfishness. We must, or it kills us!

This notion of selfishness—wanting my way—is at the heart of the Big Book's approach to the steps. Selfishness according to the dictionary is "wanting my way for my own comfort or convenience".

The Big Book, however, discusses selfishness in a broader, more generic, way—as "wanting my way", period—not only for my own comfort or convenience, and perhaps even for the best of motives.

This broader approach will become extremely important when we discuss Step Four and ask where we have been selfish in relation to other people.

The Promises of the program:

At the top of page 63 the Big Book has some promises, and some people interpret those promises as being the promises of Step Three. I've been taught that this is not the case.

Let's read those promises carefully. I'll emphasize the conditional and forward-looking parts of these promises:

> When we SINCERELY took such a position, all sorts of remarkable things followed. We had a new Employer. Being all powerful, He provided what we needed, IF we kept close to Him and performed His work well. Established on such a footing we BECAME less and less interested in ourselves, our little plans and designs. More and more we BECAME interested in seeing what we could contribute to life. AS we felt new power flow in, AS we enjoyed peace of mind, AS we discovered we could face life successfully, AS we became conscious of His presence, we BEGAN to lose our fear of today, tomorrow or the hereafter. We were reborn.

These are really the promises of the whole program, not of Step Three. They are conditional on doing the steps; and Step Three is simply the beginning—the decision to do the steps.

(Note that we have a new employer. We don't get our job description until we have recovered. See page 102 for our job description: "Your job now is to be at the place where you may be of maximum helpfulness to others". We can't do that job until we have worked the steps and recovered. The Big Book makes that clear on page 164: "But obviously you cannot transmit something you haven't got.")

Another way of proving that these are the promises of the whole program is to show that the only real promise that's made about Step Three is found at the bottom of page 63: "This was only a beginning, though if honestly and humbly made, an effect, sometimes a very great one, was felt at once." We're promised an effect of some kind. And further, look at the top of page 64: "Though our decision was a vital and crucial step, it could have little permanent effect unless at once followed by a strenuous effort to face, and to be rid of, the things in ourselves which had been blocking us."

So from a careful reading of the Big Book and in the light of the history of the steps, I think we can see that Step Three is a vital and important step, but it's not a step we spend a lot of time on. It's a step where we reflect on what brought us to our knees—the broad notion of selfishness, wanting our way regardless of the motives—and make a decision (in effect, while still on our knees!) to find a Higher Power by working the steps.

Our job is to unblock the channel between ourselves and our Higher Power deep down within us. To do that we have to clean house. To do that, therefore, we have to do Steps Four through Nine,.

Taking Step Three:

So let's say the Step Three prayer. The Big Book says that the language is optional so long as the idea is expressed, and that it is "very desirable" to say that prayer "with an understanding person".

> God, I offer myself to Thee—to build with me and to do with me as Thou wilt. Relieve me of the bondage of self, that I may better do Thy will. Take away my difficulties, that victory over them may bear witness to those I would help of Thy Power, Thy Love, and Thy Way of life. May I do Thy will always!

A beautiful prayer! We're offering ourselves to God. We want certain things to happen to us—relief from the bondage of self, difficulties taken away—not for those things to benefit US, but so that those things will help us benefit OTHERS. This is the first time the Big Book really begins to say that we need to get out of our skin and to help others.

So that's it! That's Step Three.

We don't have to be really really really ready; we simply have to make a decision. The "really really really ready" part comes if we actually start to do some work—start Step Four.

Remember that I can make a decision to travel, but I won't get anywhere if I don't get in my car and drive or buy a plane ticket and get on the plane.

Hanging by a branch:

A man falls off a cliff, and manages to catch a little branch halfway down the cliff. It starts to come off its roots.

He starts to pray: "God, I've never prayed before, but please, please, help me."

A deep voice sounds out: "I'm here, my son."

"God, is that you?"

"Yes, my son."

"Oh, God, what do I do, what do I do?"

"Let go of the branch, my son."

"Pardon me?"

"Let go of the branch, my son."

There's a long silence, and then the man speaks: "Is there anyone else up there?"

Three Frogs:

Three frogs are sitting on a log. Two make a decision to jump off a log. Five minutes pass. How many frogs are left on the log?

The answer isn't one. Nor is the answer that the third frog would have jumped along with the other two. The answer is three. The frogs just made a *decision* to jump; they didn't actually do it.

The Flash Flood:

A man is sitting on his verandah in the middle of a plain, when a police cruiser comes screeching to a halt in front of him. "Get in, Frank," says the police officer, "there's going to be a flash flood, and it's going to go higher than your house!"

"No thanks," says Frank, "I've put my trust and reliance upon God." The cruiser drives off.

An hour later, the water has gone to the top of the first storey of the house. Frank is looking out the second-storey window, and a boat comes along side. "Get in, Frank," says the person piloting the boat, "it's going to get worse!"

"No thanks," says Frank, "I've put my trust and reliance upon God." The boat goes away.

An hour later, the water is over the roof, and Frank is hanging onto the television antenna. A helicopter comes by and lets down a ladder. "It's getting higher, climb on!"

"No thanks," says Frank, "I've put my trust and reliance upon God." The helicopter flies off.

Frank drowns, goes to heaven, and demands to see the Big Guy. "Where were you?" he asks angrily.

God says, "I sent a car, a boat, and a helicopter!"

The lottery:

A man kneels in his sparse bedroom and prays: "God, I'm going to be praying to you day and night until Saturday afternoon. I need to win the lottery. Not the million dollars, but just $40,000.00. And it's not for me, but for the benefit of a particular charity that needs it right away. So I'm going to pray and pray."

Saturday afternoon comes. He's been praying for the whole week. "Just one more hour," he says, "just one more. Please, God, let me win just $40,000.00."

The blue sky suddenly is completely clouded over. There's lots of thunder and lightning, but no rain. A shaft of sunlight streams onto his face. A deep and exasperated voice says, "Buy a ticket!"

We therefore don't have to wait to see if our will and our lives have ACTUALLY been turned over to God—we've only DECIDED to do that, but we haven't as yet done anything to accomplish that!

So please don't hang around waiting for something—just keep on doing the steps!

Remember the Big Book's discussion of Step Two: we are blocked off from our Higher Power deep down within us.

The Big Book constantly reminds us that "Faith without works is dead." We have to take action, and that action will be cleaning house—Steps Four through Nine.

Cleaning house will remove those things that block us from our Higher Power, and the promises of Step Nine will show us that by that time our will and our life will have been turned over to our Higher Power!

Questions:

Here are some questions:

- If you look at your frustrations and feelings about the past, do you see how they arose because things just didn't happen your way?
- Do you see yourself as the actor who wants to be the director/producer?
- Can you think of situations when you wanted things to go your way for the best of motives? How did you feel when they didn't go your way? And how do you feel now about those things? Are they settled now? Are you serene about them? Or do they still bother you in some way?
- Can you think of situations when you wanted things to go your way for motives which you consider to be self-centered? How did you feel when they didn't go your way? And how do you feel now about those things? Are they settled now? Are you serene about them? Or do they still bother you in some way?
- Can you see how wanting things to go your way is blocking you off from your Higher Power?
- Are you ready to make a decision to search for a Higher Power by cleaning house and thus unblocking you from your Higher Power? If you are, find an understanding person and say the Step Three Prayer!

Now let's rush on to Step Four!

> My experience has been that there is no need to add to the Big Book's approach by bringing in concepts from the AA 12 & 12 (as even Joe and Charlie do) or from anywhere else. Many people have achieved recovery quickly and efficiently by doing the Step Four inventory the Big Book way. For more discussion, see page 36.

> On page 62,the Big Book says:
>
> > Sometimes they hurt us, seemingly without provocation, but we invariably find that at some time in the past we have made decisions based on self which later placed us in a position to be hurt.
>
> This is a sentence which can easily be misinterpreted as somehow saying that we have brought on or are responsible for our own misfortunes, but I know that's not the case. If I were abused as a child, no one can say (and certainly the Big Book wouldn't say) that I somehow deserved the abuse; but if I'm grown up now, and that abuse still hurts me, even if the abuser is dead, then I have indeed "sometime in the past made decisions based on self which later placed [me] in a position to be hurt"!
>
> I think that's all the Big Book is saying. If I live my life believing that nothing good has happened to me, then I will live my life in unhappiness, and block myself off from my Higher Power, and continue to be a compulsive eater. If I can find a way to give up my wish to have life go my way, then I can finally live life as it should be lived!

Step Four:

I think you'll find that Step Four the Big Book way is really very simple and very fast, much simpler and faster than many of the Step Four methods that are popular in OA.

Last chapter we discussed Step Three. We learned that from the Big Book perspective, it is simply making a decision to go on with the Twelve Steps. "This was only a beginning," the Big Book says on page 63. And it says further, on page 64: "Though our decision [Step Three] was a vital and crucial step, it could have little permanent effect unless AT ONCE followed by a strenuous effort to face, and to be rid of, the things in ourselves which had been blocking us."

In Step Two we learned that our Higher Power, which is deep down within us, was blocked off from us ("obscured", the Big Book says) because of calamities, pomp, and worship of other things (page 55). In Step Three we made a decision to place our will and our lives into the care of our Higher Power. What we have to do now is to be rid of those things in ourselves which have been blocking us from our Higher Power. When we get rid of the things that block us from our Higher Power, we will find that our Higher Power enters into our lives. The task at hand is to get rid of the blocks.

Step Four BEGINS this process of unblocking. It is NOT, however, the entire process. That process is Steps Four through Nine. The Big Book promises recovery by the end of Step Nine. And by virtue of Steps Ten and Eleven, that process continues through our entire lives.

That Step Four is not the entire inventory process is made clear by the discussion on pages 64 and 65. "Therefore, we STARTED upon a personal inventory. This was Step Four."

The Big Book compares our personal inventory with a business inventory. It says that the purpose of a business inventory is "to discover the truth about the stock-in-trade." In a business inventory, we look at the good and the bad of our business—what sells and what doesn't sell, what's in good shape and what's in bad shape.

As the Big Book points out, *one* of the objects of a commercial inventory "is to disclose damaged or unsalable goods, to get rid of them promptly and without regret." And the Big Book says, "We did exactly the same thing with our lives. First, we searched out the flaws in our make-up which caused our failure."

This makes clear, I think, that the purpose of the Step Four inventory is NOT to look at BOTH the good and the bad of our lives, something that many Step Four inventory processes suggest.

No, the purpose of the Big Book way of doing an inventory is *solely* "to disclose damaged or unsalable goods" (Steps Four and Five) and "to get rid of them promptly and without regret" (Steps Six, Seven, Eight, and Nine).

Thus the inventory process is Steps Four through Nine. This will become significant when we discuss Step Ten.

Note that at the end of the discussion of Step Four, the Big Book says that we have made "an inventory of [our] grosser handicaps". It's very clear that in Step Four we deal with the big problems, and that we leave the refining for Steps Ten and Eleven. The Big Book continues to push us to do the steps quickly so we can reach recovery.

Overview:

Let's start with the overview. The Big Book suggests that in Step Three we were "convinced that self, manifested in various ways, was what had defeated us" (page 64). The Big Book has three aspects of self that it wants us to look at.

The first is resentments, and we'll deal with them in this and the next chapter. We will find, I think, that a resentment is, in its broadest sense, the concept that "the past didn't go my way".

The second aspect of self, which we'll deal with the chapter after next, is fear. We will find, I think, that a fear is, in its broadest sense, the concept that "the future won't go my way".

The third aspect of self, which we'll also deal with the chapter after next, is sex conduct. We will find, I think, that the purpose of dealing with sex conduct is to figure out how we should handle the most difficult of relationships in order to have good relationships of every kind.

So the Big Book's ordering of Step Four is basically dealing with the Past, dealing with the Future, and then learning how to live in the present with other people. It's very simple and very powerful!

At www.oabigbook.info you can find examples of filled-out forms which might help you fill out your forms. You can find these examples in the Appendices to this book as well.

Step Four—Resentments:

So let's start with resentments — what the Big Book calls "the 'number one' offender." (page 64)

What is a resentment? It is something on our minds that we resent. Now "resentment" is broader than "anger". It includes anger, but it goes much farther. Its Latin roots mean "to feel over and over", and it's best described as anything that's living rent-free in your mind, things that you regret, things that anger you or that frustrate you, things that you wish had happened or hadn't happened, the what-ifs or if-onlys of our lives.

You can consider a resentment as something or somebody that you're angry at because it occupies your mind. In a sense, then, you're angry at people to whom you've done wrongs, because your guilt continues to occupy your mind. That sense of resentment allows you to broaden the concept of anger beyond the dictionary definition.

In one way or another, a resentment, then, is that what happened in the past just didn't go your way. It's what we discovered in Step Three—that we want to be in charge, and that life hasn't gone our way.

The first instruction the Big Book gives is to list "people, institutions or principles with whom we were angry" (Page 64). It is true that the Big Book uses the word "angry". I can only suggest that listing people, institutions, or principles that you resent (or that you are "angry" at because they occupy your mind) is very very helpful.

People are people. You make a list of people who are living rent-free in your mind.

Institutions are institutions—groups of people.

Principles, however, are not defined in the Big Book and are not easy to define. I find that it's very helpful to consider "principles" as meaning "ideas that seem to be true that bother me". Here are some examples:

- I'll never get thin.
- There will always be terrible suffering in this world.
- I can never eat french fries again.
- Life sucks, and then you die.
- People ignore me.
- I'll never amount to anything.
- This program will never work.
- I'm fat and ugly and unlovable.
- No one understands my pain.

Don't put yourself down—but do put down principles *about* yourself that bother you. That will give you true insight into issues relating to you.

Filling out the resentment form:

COLUMN ONE:

The first instruction is simply to make a list. If you use the form available on the web site, you'll see that each form has room for three names of people or institutions or principles. Since the second column is going to have much more writing on it, if you know that a particular name or institution or principle is going to have a lot of writing in the second column, you could reserve a whole page for that particular item.

Making this list is relatively simple. The question is "what is on your mind right now?" It's not "what has been on your mind in the past?" Therefore you're just putting things down that you're conscious of, not things that you think you should put down. You may have had some traumatic things happen to you but have put them to rest and don't think about them. If that's true, why put them down? We're just putting down what's affecting us now.

I've put down very serious items, like my wife and my parents and my children, like Hitler and certain politicians and murderers, like ex-girlfriends and the man I trusted who lied to me, and very minor things, like people who don't spell words correctly or that person who cut me off at the intersection.

I also put down people I've harmed, because I continue to think about that harm and feel guilty about it, and that's a resentment as well.

I have found that if I write my list in an evening I will remember some more things in the morning.

COLUMN TWO:

The second instruction is to ask "why we were angry" (page 64), or what "our injuries" were (page 65). An example is given at the bottom of page 65 for what we write in this column. We are to write

Clear Form

The "BIG BOOK'S" Way to Be Rid of Resentment (pages 63—67)

INSTRUCTIONS:		Affects my: (3)						DON'T FORGET THIS!	Core Character Defects (4)
Study from the bottom of page 63 to the end of page 65 and **then** follow its instructions: a) List all people, institutions and principles (Column 1) from **top to bottom**. b) List all "causes" (Column 2), **top to bottom**. c) Do all six instincts in Column 3 from **top to bottom for each "cause"**. d) Consider the first three columns carefully. e) Then, complete Column 4 from **top to bottom.**		Self-Esteem	Security (Pkt. Books)	Ambitions	Personal Relations	Sex Relations	Is any fear involved?	**Study** from the bottom of page 65 to end of the 3rd paragraph on page 67, and **then** follow the instructions. *Go to each person who has harmed you or someone and say "_____ is spiritually sick." Don't forget to say the Resentment Prayer (Lines 3-5, page 67), "God, please help me show _____ the same tolerance, pity and patience I would cheerfully grant a sick friend" for each and every person who has harmed you, themselves or someone else in Column 1 prior to starting Column 4.*	"Putting out of our minds the wrongs others have done, **[use fold lines to cover Columns 2 and 3]** we resolutely looked for our own mistakes. Where had we been selfish, dishonest, self-seeking and frightened? . . . [D]isregard the other person involved entirely. Where were we to blame? . . . When we saw our faults we **listed** them. We placed them before us in **black and white**. We admitted our wrongs honestly and were willing to set these matters straight." (page 67)
I'm resentful at: (1)	**The causes: (2)**								
									Selfish:
									Dishonest:
									Self-Seeking:
									Frightened:
									Selfish:
									Dishonest:
									Self-Seeking:
									Frightened:
									Selfish:
									Dishonest:
									Self-Seeking:
									Frightened:

Clear Form

THE BIG BOOK'S WAY OF REMOVING FEARS (PP. 67 & 68)

INSTRUCTIONS: **a)** Study from the bottom of page 67 to the bottom of page 68 in the book *Alcoholics Anonymous.* **b)** Complete column 1 (listing whom or what I am fearful of), **from top to bottom**. **c)** Complete the remaining columns from **top to bottom** for each fear in column 1. Remember that "we are now on a different basis; the basis of trusting and relying upon God. We trust infinite God rather than our finite selves. . . . Just to the extent that we do as we think He would have us, and humbly rely on Him, does He enable us to match calamity with serenity" (page 68).

I'm fearful of: (1)	**Why do I have the fear? (2)**	**Where was my trust & reliance? (3)**		**Did self reliance work? (4)**		**Fear Prayer: "God, please remove my fear and direct my attention to what you would have me be" (5)**	**What would God have you be?** Write out your answer to that question for each and every fear listed. (6)
		Infinite God	My Finite Self	Yes	No	COMPLETED FEAR PRAYER? ☐	
		Infinite God	My Finite Self	Yes	No	COMPLETED FEAR PRAYER? ☐	
		Infinite God	My Finite Self	Yes	No	COMPLETED FEAR PRAYER? ☐	
		Infinite God	My Finite Self	Yes	No	COMPLETED FEAR PRAYER? ☐	
		Infinite God	My Finite Self	Yes	No	COMPLETED FEAR PRAYER? ☐	
		Infinite God	My Finite Self	Yes	No	COMPLETED FEAR PRAYER? ☐	
		Infinite God	My Finite Self	Yes	No	COMPLETED FEAR PRAYER? ☐	
		Infinite God	My Finite Self	Yes	No	COMPLETED FEAR PRAYER? ☐	

THE BIG BOOK'S WAY TO "SENSIBLY OVERHAUL" OUR OWN SEX CONDUCT (Pages 68—70)

INSTRUCTIONS: a) Study from the bottom of page 68 to the end of third paragraph on page 70. **b)** Fill in Column 1from top to bottom. **c)** Do Column 2 **from top to bottom. d)** Fill in each of the remaining columns **from top to bottom.** *Do not work across the page from left to right.* Don't forget the **Sex Prayer** ("God, please mold my ideals and help me to live up to them") on page 69, and the Big Book's **Sex Meditation** ("God, please show me what to do about this [each] specific matter") on page 69. "The right answer will come if we want it". This will shape a "sane and sound ideal for our future sex life" (page 69). Be sure to restudy what happens if we "fall short of the chosen ideal and stumble" on page 70. Be sure to continue to pray the "Earnest" prayers from page 70 (on the right hand side of this page) for ongoing guidance, strength, sanity, and the right ideal. **Clear Form Data**

Whom did I hurt? (1)	Where was I (2)	Did I arouse: (3)	Where was I at fault, what should I have done instead? (4)	Was each relation? (5)	Sex Prayer Page 69(6)	Sex Meditation Page 69(7)	The Earnest Prayers page 70
Selfish: Dishonest: Inconsiderate:		Jealousy? Suspicion? Bitterness?		SELFISH Yes No	"God, please mold my ideals and help me to live up to them." ☐	"God, please show me what to do about this[each] specific matter" ☐	**W**e earnestly pray for: **T**he right ideal **G**uidance in each questionable situation
Selfish: Dishonest: Inconsiderate:		Jealousy? Suspicion? Bitterness?		SELFISH Yes No	"God, please mold my ideals and help me to live up to them." ☐	"God, please show me what to do about this[each] specific matter" ☐	**S**anity **T**he strength to do the right thing **I**f sex is troublesome, we throw ourselves the harder into helping others.
Selfish: Dishonest: Inconsiderate:		Jealousy? Suspicion? Bitterness?		SELFISH Yes No	"God, please mold my ideals and help me to live up to them." ☐	"God, please show me what to do about this[each] specific matter" ☐	**W**e think of their needs and work for them. **T**his takes us out of ourselves. **I**t quiets the imperious urge, when to yield would mean heartache.

short and to-the-point description of the various things that put these people or these institutions or these principles in our minds. We need to write only enough so that we know what we are talking about. We're not filling out this second column for anyone but ourselves.

Let me give some examples.

Beside Hitler, for example, I can put:

- responsible for the deaths of millions of people
- furthered the cause of anti-Semitism
- is still a hero to some people
- created conditions that created problems for my growing up

Beside an ex-girlfriend, for example (and this is ONLY an example!), I could put:

- didn't love me enough
- used me
- I used her
- that one day when . . .
- I still think of her
- if only . . .

Beside the institution of government, for example, I could put:

- doesn't accomplish anything
- I don't get involved enough
- people are still suffering

Beside the principle of "I'll never get thin", for example, I could put:

- I'll never be attractive to the opposite sex
- I'll die early
- I'll waste those pants I've been saving for ten years!
- I don't want to give up food badly enough

You can see the kind of things we fill out in the second column. The object is to have as many points as possible, but there's no need to go into any details on each point.

COLUMN THREE:

The third instruction is to ask ourselves "Was it our self-esteem, our security, our ambitions, our personal, or sex relations, which had been interfered with?" (page 65). (You'll note at the bottom of page 64, a similar set of categories, but with "pocketbooks"—wallets or purses—instead of "security".) The resentment form has separate sub-columns for each one of these concepts. As well, because the example at the bottom of page 65 has "fear" in that third column as well, the form has a separate sub-column for fear.

Self-esteem means how I feel about myself. Security means how safe I feel, including financially safe. Ambitions means what I want out of life. Personal relations, sex relations, and fear, are obvious.

So for each one of the "causes" (column two) we put check-marks where each one of these sub-categories has been affected.

Using the Hitler example above, for instance:

- *responsible for the deaths of millions of people.* Doesn't affect my self-esteem and sex relations, does affect my security, my ambitions, and my personal relationships, and is associated with fear.
- *furthered the cause of anti-Semitism.* Does affect my self-esteem, security, ambitions, personal relationships, and is associated with fear; doesn't affect my sex relations.
- *is still a hero to some people.* Doesn't affect my self-esteem, my personal relations, my sex relations; does affect my security, my ambitions, and my fear.
- *created conditions that created problems for my growing up*. . . . etc.

Using the "I'll never be thin" example above, for instance:

- *I'll never be attractive to the opposite sex.* Affects my self-esteem, ambitions, personal and sex relations and fear; doesn't affect my security.
- *I'll die early.* Doesn't affect my self-esteem, personal or sex relations; affects my ambitions and fear and security.
- *I'll waste those pants I've been saving for ten years!* Affects my security (pocketbooks), but doesn't affect anything else.
- *I don't want to give up food badly enough*. . . . etc.

So you can see that filling out these sub-columns involves some thinking about each particular point in column two and how it is affecting me.

The Big Book says about this process: "We went back through our lives. Nothing counted but thoroughness and honesty" (page 65).

I don't know how long it will take each one of you to do this, but it shouldn't take a very long time. Even if you end up with 200 names of people and institutions and principles, and even if you put down four or five points about most of them, and ten or twenty points about some of them, that's not going to take more than a total of ten or fifteen hours. Granted, you may want to take some time to do this, to think about things, but the object is to write down what's on your mind, not what's lurking in your sub-conscious mind. Column one is naming; column two is venting; and column three begins an analysis.

EXAMINING CAREFULLY WHAT WE'VE DONE:

Now here's what the Big Book says after we finish these three columns. "The first thing apparent was that this world and its people were often quite wrong" (pages 64 to 65).

It is truly an amazing feeling after filling out these three columns to see how many check-marks we have put down. We begin to see that the most important things about ourselves—how we feel about ourselves (self-esteem), how safe we feel (security), how frustrated we feel (ambitions), how we relate to others (personal relations), how we relate sexually to others (sex relations), and how fearful we are—are being controlled by other people and institutions and abstract concepts. No wonder we're not happy. And no wonder we eat. The Big Book says:

> It is plain that a life which includes deep resentment leads only to futility and unhappiness. To the precise extent that we permit these, do we squander the hours that might have been worth while. But with the alcoholic, whose hope is the maintenance and growth of a spiritual experience, this business of resentment is infinitely grave. We found that it is fatal. For when harboring such feelings we shut ourselves off from the sunlight of the Spirit. The insanity of alcohol returns and we drink again. And with us, to drink is to die. If we were to live, we had to be free of anger. The grouch and the brainstorm were not for us. They may be the dubious luxury of normal men, but for alcoholics these things are poison. (page 65)

How true those words are! Any life—alcoholic or compulsive eater or not—which includes deep resentment tends to futility and unhappiness, because we waste time that we could have used for something else. But for us compulsive eaters, deep resentment is absolutely fatal, because "we shut ourselves off" from our higher power, and we go back to eating. We have to be free of anger/resentment, that "dubious luxury of normal men".

As you fill the form out, I think you will begin to see how brilliant and how deep it is. (I showed it to a psychiatrist once who was overwhelmed by it.)

- First column, we just list on paper things that are bugging us.
- Second column, we write out why they're bugging us.
- Third column, we begin to see how the things that are bugging us are actually killing us. People who did us wrong continue to harm us. People we did harm to harm us. Ideas that we have are killing us. No wonder we're blocked off from our higher power!

You can see how this form gives us hope. We're moving from the things that BOTHER us to to the things that are BLOCKING us from our higher power! There's hope just around the corner! As the Big Book says at page 65, this list holds "the key to the future"!

Questions:

Here are some questions. The whole of Step Four is answering questions, of course.

- What's on your mind that's bugging you?
- Are the reasons that these things are bothering you affecting much of your life? Do they affect how you feel about yourself, how safe you feel, how frustrated you feel, how good or bad your relations (personal or sexual) are, and how full of fear you are?
- Can you see that these things are blocking you from the sunlight of the spirit?

Resentments Continued:

Last chapter I discussed the first three columns of the resentment form. These are the columns actually depicted on page 65 of the Big Book. Many people (including me for the first six years in the program) assumed that those three columns are the only columns in the resentment form.

In fact, there is a fourth column, and it turns out that this fourth column is the most important one of all! The first three columns are actually simply PREPARATIONS for the fourth column.

The essential Fourth Column:

Let's remember that the purpose of Step Four is to identify those parts of ourselves which are blocking us from our higher power. We have decided, in Step Three, to turn our will and our lives over to the care of God as we understand God. That decision means that we have to discover what defects of character block us from our higher power. The fourth column of the resentment form is in fact our analysis of those defects of character.

Dealing with things that bother us:

But before we can look at our defects of character, we have to deal with all the things that bother us—those aspects of the past that haven't gone our way.

The check-marks in the third column are very effective graphic representations of our paralysis. And they help us to convince ourselves that the things in our past which bother us—our resentments—have the power to kill us, because so long as we felt our resentments, the third column showed us that we felt badly about ourselves (self-esteem), we felt unsafe (security), we felt thwarted and frustrated (ambitions), our personal and sex relations were deeply affected, and we were full of fear. How could we live life positively if these very deep emotions were being controlled by how we feel about the past?

The Big Book tells us that we should go back to our list, "for it [holds] the key to the future" (page 65). If we can master our resentments, then we can look at our own flaws.

Our biggest problem is, of course, with people who have wronged us, people who have done things which we wish they hadn't done. If we can't overcome our resentments against them, we will not be able to see our part, our flaws.

Here the Big Book gives very cryptic but clear instructions:

> This was our course: We realized that the people who wronged us were perhaps spiritually sick. Though we did not like their symptoms and the way these disturbed us, they, like ourselves, were sick too. We asked God to help us show them the same tolerance, pity, and patience that we would cheerfully grant a sick friend. (pages 65-66)

What does it mean to say that the people who wronged us were, "like ourselves", also sick? What is a spiritual sickness?

How do we treat people as spiritually sick?

We excuse people all the time. We understand it and often instantly forgive people who have neurological disorders (like Tourette's Syndrome) or brain tumours, or who are in constant pain, if they snap at us or insult us. We realize that it isn't really their fault. Things are going on inside them that make their reactions to life beyond their control. If I were in constant pain, I think I'd be pretty grouchy most of the time.

Can we not look at people who have wronged us as being in spiritual pain? Let's look at the history of the people who have wronged us. Can we not see somewhere in their upbringing, or in their life experiences, or in how they relate to other people, that they are sick?

How many people who have committed sexual or physical violence were themselves recipients of abuse? How many "bad" parents were themselves the product of "bad" parenting? Don't many people do bad things for reasons which they think are valid? Isn't there a sickness to be seen in those people?

And what right do I have to be righteous? Haven't I done bad things for reasons which I thought were valid? Maybe not as bad as these people, but in reality, they're not so much worse than I am.

Page 552 (third and fourth edition) of the Big Book contains a suggestion for dealing with resentments we find overwhelmingly difficult to overcome. The suggestion is that we pray for those we resent that "everything you want for yourself be given to them—their health, their prosperity, their happiness"; that we do this whether we want to or not.

The amazing thing about this suggestion is that it requires us first of all to figure out what we want for ourselves. When I did this, I realized that what I really wanted for my self was serenity, a sense of usefulness, an ability to love and to be loved.

And when I prayed for the people I hated, something hit me in the face—that wonderful blinding flash of the obvious!—and that was that none of the people I hated were serene, were useful, or were able to love and to be loved. They led lives based on fear or mistrust of other people. They were cruel or dishonest or hurt others (including me). How could they ever have serenity? How could they ever be useful? How could they ever love or be loved? Even if they thought they were happy, they were living superficial and sad lives.

Thus the more harm they did in this world, the more they cut themselves off from the sunlight of the spirit, the less human they became, the more harm they did to themselves.

That is spiritual sickness. That is pitiful. I began not to hate them but to pity them. Certainly I hated what they had done, not simply to me but to others. But I saw that every wrong move they made, every hurt they created, was a nail in their own coffin as well. They did harm to themselves by doing harm to others.

I was thus able to deal with such difficult people on my list as Hitler and others who have been responsible for horrible deeds in this world. By the time they committed all those deeds, they had rendered themselves so sub-human that it seemed impossible for them ever to regain their humanity. The things they did were horrible; and the "things" they became were horrible too. You can't blame a dog or a cat for doing damage in your house. And these people were more like animals (not that I'm saying that dogs or cats could do what these people did!) than like humans.

As well, I was and am willing to admit that I am not perfect! I clearly have a spiritual sickness—the Big Book has convinced me of that. That spiritual sickness consists at the very least of my wish to be in charge of life, and my everlasting frustration that life hasn't gone my way and is likely never to go my way.

> The author of the story "Freedom from Bondage", where the page 552 resentment prayer is found, gives credit in a talk she gave in 1973 in Oxnard, California, to an article in *Liberty* providing a condensation of Norman Vincent Peale's book, *A Guide to Confident Living*.

By definition that's a spiritual sickness! If I'm willing to understand myself, then I have to be willing to understand others.

So these few sentences from the bottom of page 66 to the top of page 67 really helped change my attitudes to people who had been controlling my life because of the things they had done to me or to my loved ones or to humanity in general. I was able to look at them as extremely damaged people, and to feel pity and sadness for them. In effect, they had become "beneath contempt".

Moreover I began to see something that will become extremely important for the fourth column of this resentment form. If I accept that the more harm they did to me or others, the more harm they did to themselves, then I am forced to accept that allowing them to continue to do harm allowed them to do harm to themselves. Thus I began to get an insight into the character defect of dishonesty, which I'll talk about in a few paragraphs.

So we look at these people (column one), "their symptoms" (column two), "and the way these disturbed us" (column three). We find that these people were sick too. And we're given a prayer to say. "We asked God to help us show them the same tolerance, pity, and patience that we would cheerfully grant a sick friend." There's the prayer: "God, please help me show ______ the same tolerance, pity, and patience, that I would cheerfully grant a sick friend."

Our four defects of character:

Now that we have said that prayer about each person on our list who has harmed us or others,

> On page 67, after providing the instructions for Step Four, the Big Book goes on to suggest ways in which we deal with people who bother us in the future:
>
> "When a person offended [the original manuscript actually said "*next* offended"] we said to ourselves, 'This is a sick man. How can I be helpful to him? God save me from being angry. Thy will be done.'"
>
> As well, the Big Book suggests ways of dealing with these people in the future—avoiding retaliation or argument. Neither this prayer nor these suggestions are part of the Step Four instructions. They are guides to living.

we're ready to look at our own mistakes. Here are the Big Book's instructions (page 67):

> Referring to our list again. Putting out of our minds the wrongs others had done, we resolutely looked for our own mistakes. Where had we been selfish, dishonest, self-seeking and frightened? Though a situation had not been entirely our fault, we tried to disregard the other person involved entirely. Where were we to blame?

So the instructions on the form are pretty literal. To put out of our minds the wrongs others had done, we fold the paper over to cover columns two and three, leaving us with columns one and four.

Covering up columns two and three:

Why do we cover up columns two and three?

It's not simply because the Big Book tells us to put out of our minds the wrongs others have done us, and that's what's in columns two and three—at least for those people who have done us wrong.

It's because we must now focus on where we were at fault. That requires a look at the *entire* relationship between those people, principles, and institutions listed in column one and ourselves. What columns two and three represent is not the *entire* relationship, but simply the *particular* issues that came to mind when we started upon our inventory.

Now that we've been able to accept those who have wronged us as spiritually sick, now that we're focusing on our own contributions to the problems, we are entering a new way of looking at things. That requires us to cover up columns two and three.

We don't forget about the matters that might have appeared in columns two and three. Very often—but not always—those matters will surface in column four. *Sometimes*, however, those matters will have disappeared and completely new and striking insights will surface.

So we cover up columns two and three and then look at the people, institutions, and principles, on our lists (column one) and ask ourselves four simple questions: Where have I been selfish? Where have I been dishonest? Where have I been self-seeking? Where have I been frightened?

Definitions:

What do these words mean? This is the best I've come up with.

SELFISH:

Selfish has already been defined very broadly by the Big Book in its discussion of Step Three. Selfish means not only what the dictionary says it means—wanting things my way for my own purposes or comfort—but it also means something broader than that. It means wanting things my way period, regardless of my motives. (See the discussion of Step Three for more details.)

DISHONEST:

Dishonest certainly means telling untruths, lying, defrauding, deceiving. And the recipient of the dishonesty isn't always another person. It can be me! I can be fooling myself about reality.

Beyond that, for a people-pleaser like me, another aspect of dishonesty is "not telling the truth when the truth should be told". If I continued in a relationship, for instance, in which harm was being done to me (and I've been in some destructive relationships, although nothing even close to the kind of abuse I've heard described in the rooms of OA), or if I've seen injustices being done and said nothing (and that's happened much more often), am I not being dishonest by not speaking the truth, by not saying, "Wait a minute, this is wrong!"?

There may be understandable reasons for doing this, but isn't that a character flaw; and isn't that ultimately dishonesty too?

So there are three kinds of dishonesty: telling untruths to others, telling untruths to myself, and not telling the truth when the truth should be told.

SELF-SEEKING:

Self-seeking is more difficult to define. The Big Book rarely uses it. A dictionary will use the word "selfish" to describe "self-seeking", which isn't really helpful to us. My best understanding of the word comes from breaking it down: "Seeking my self" in others. It's like self-esteem. How does this person, institution, or principle in column one define how I feel about myself?

We can also understand it by asking whether with this person or principle or institution it was all about us or whether it was about the other. In that context, self-seeking is putting our sense of selves forward. It's also not being considerate of others, because we're thinking of ourselves.

I've found those concepts to be very helpful questions to ask, so that's how I interpret the word "self-seeking".

FRIGHTENED:

Frightened asks us how and why we felt any fear in relation to the people, institutions, or principles in column one.

Those are the four character defects the Big Book discloses with respect to resentments. We'll see that no more are added by the fear and sex conduct parts of Step Four. We can see now that these four character defects completely define our problem.

Applying the definitions:

Selfish: I'm selfish. At the very least, I wish the people, institutions, or principles that I set out in column one just didn't exist or hadn't happened or hadn't done to me what they did or I didn't do what I did to them. I just wish the past was different. I wish people hadn't died or got sick. I wish people didn't suffer as they're suffer. I wish the world were a better place. That's selfish, the Big Book way—I want my way rather than what is. But I will also find that there is much of me that is selfish the dictionary way. I wish that the people, institutions, or principles in column one hadn't happened because of the pain or the humiliation or the lack of security or the bad relationships or the bitterness or the guilt or the . . . .—in other words, I wish that these things hadn't happened because they don't make me feel good. And I wish that the people, institutions, or principles in column one would be different so I could feel happier, so I could be acknowledged as the great person I really am, so I could make lots of money, so I could buy things for my own comfort, so I . . .

Dishonest:I'm dishonest. I haven't accepted that some people aren't capable of acting any differently than the way they did. I don't speak up when I should for fear of hurting people's feelings. I haven't left relationships that were harming both myself and the person who was harming me because I thought I could change the person (as if I were in control!). I have told stories about other people (gossiped) because I wanted people to like me and not to like them, or not to have good feelings about them. And I have also told untruths to myself, persuading myself that the past could be different, that certain people could change if I only did this or that, that somehow people who did me harm were conscious of what they were doing or were really making rational choices instead of just doing what they learned from their own sad experiences. And I have also told untruths to others.

Self-seeking: And self-seeking? Wow. I have let so many people and situations define how I feel about myself. I have sought after a definition of myself in others. If you like me, then maybe I'm likable. If you don't like me, then you're probably really smart, because you can see below the surface. One bad evaluation out of a hundred is the one that I focus on.

Fear: And full of fear! Afraid that people will find out what I've done. Afraid that people won't respect or like or admire me. Afraid that I won't get what I want. Afraid I'll lose what I have. Afraid of confronting someone. Afraid for my life.

It's worth mulling over all these ideas and applying them to your situation.

How the Steps give us back our lives:

One (inaccurate) criticism of Twelve Step programs that we hear a lot is that the Twelve Steps teach us that it's all in our attitude, that we are to blame for misfortunes that happen to us. I don't think that's true at all.

The Twelve Steps certainly provide us a way of getting out of being a victim. But they also, through their emphasis on rigorous honesty, teach us that we must be honest in our dealings with others.

That means that we say to people that what they're doing is wrong; and we say that not just because they may be hurting us or others, but because they're hurting THEMSELVES! It's our duty to tell the truth when the truth should be told.

Although I have never suffered the kind of abuse that other OAers have suffered, I have had the privilege of sponsoring a number of people who have suffered tremendous abuse, sexual and physical, both as children and as adults. They have all confirmed the concepts contained in this discussion of Step Four.

As children, most of them were, of course, silent. Or as abused spouses they kept in the relationship far longer than they should have. They don't look at the past with guilt and beat themselves up for not having spoken up earlier. (As children, they might not have been believed anyway!)

They simply look at the past as something for them to learn from, so that they won't be victims again. And their "amend" ultimately turns out to be something positive, sometimes a change in themselves and their approach to problems in the future, sometimes disclosing things that they feel should have been disclosed. But they become different people as a result, and that is what the steps are all about. We'll talk more about that when we discuss Steps Eight and Nine.

I hope you can see how freeing this approach to resentments is.

Overview:

In **column one** we start by just listing them. This serves a useful purpose. We get things out of our minds and onto a paper; this in itself will at times get rid of the resentment.

Then in **column two** we list all the particulars about why they're on our mind, and we thus get to analyze what exactly is going on; that in itself yields interesting results. Sometimes when we put this down on paper, we realize how some of the reasons are silly, and they begin to leave us.

Then in **column three** we see how all those things that bother us are affecting us to the core—how we feel about ourselves, how safe we feel, how frustrated we are, how our personal and sex relations are suffering, how full of fear we are. The checkmarks are graphic illustrations of how we are completely enslaved to our reaction to life!

These first three columns show us why we are in the grip of compulsive eating. How could we possibly think we could be so sane as to remember constantly that we can't eat certain foods? No, we're just full of frustration and self-pity, and that's what's killing us. As long as we're filled with frustration and self-pity, our minds can't be clear.

We need to be full of a higher power, but instead all these things that we resent have become a higher power to us. We have to be rid of them.

We have to deal with those people who have done us harm. We do that by understanding their own sickness and praying to give them the same tolerance, pity, and patience we would cheerfully grant a sick friend.

Now, in **column four**, we're finally ready to look at our own part. We analyze each one of the people, institutions, or principles we resent in light of our own character defects. And we begin to see tremendous patterns that have clearly affected us and our lives. We begin to see how we have harmed other people, EVEN those who have harmed us. We begin to see where we could change!

Questions:

So some questions:

- Are you spiritually sick? How?
- Are you able to look at people who have harmed you as spiritually sick? In what way?
- If you're trying page 552, exactly what do you want out of your life? What would you like for yourself?
- Do those people who have harmed you have anything like what you want to have for yourself?
- Do you see your selfishness, dishonesty, self-seeking, and fear? What patterns do you see in your relationships with others in that regard?
- Do you see how these four character defects are blocking you off from the sunlight of the spirit?

Those of you aware of Joe and Charlie, the AA Big Book scholars and experts, will see some differences between the Step 4 described here and their suggested Step 4. They acknowledge that they go beyond the Big Book's instructions and incorporate ideas from AA's 12 & 12.

Joe and Charlie define "resentment" almost wholly in terms of anger, and therefore their resentments list does not contain things that would be on a resentment list if you accept, as I've been taught, that a resentment is something I wish were not on my mind—a much broader concept.

Thus Joe and Charlie have a fourth form—harm done to others—because using their definition of resentment, the harm I have done to others wouldn't be a resentment.

My experience has been that if you use a broader understanding of resentments, you don't require a fourth form.

There's another aspect as well. The Resentment form isolates our four main character defects—selfishness, dishonesty, self-seeking, and fear. The Fear and Sex Conduct forms *begin* with those defects and bring us to another level—how to act properly. The Fear form asks us what God would have us be in relation to our fears. The Sex Conduct Form deals with selfishness and dishonesty (and with self-seeking as being inconsiderate of others) in particular relationships and asks us what we should have done instead in order to act properly from now on.

The Big Book's approach to fears and sex conduct, therefore, is quite different from Joe and Charlie's approach. Not to say that it's better or worse, but I think it's important to show the differences. My experience is that if you do Step 4 as honestly as you can, it doesn't matter HOW you do it!

Step Four—Fears:

If resentments are basically "The past didn't go my way", then fears are basically "The future won't go my way." You cannot feel fear about something that has happened in the past. Fear is always an emotion that comes from imagining what will happen and not wanting that to happen.

The Big Book at page 67 says that fear "somehow touches about every aspect of our lives. It set in motion trains of circumstances which brought us misfortune we felt we didn't deserve."

The instructions are pretty clear, and the form makes them even clearer.

Filling out the Fear Form:

First "we put them on paper, even though we had no resentment in connection with them" (68).

Column One:

So we set out all the fears we have, including those we discovered in the resentment form, both in column 3 (where we asked whether fear was involved) and in column 4 (where we asked ourselves where we were frightened), as well as fears that didn't make it to the resentment list because we didn't think about them all the time.

I have put down some standard fears—fears of death, of pain, of financial insecurity, of something bad happening to loved ones, of not being happy, of not losing weight—and fears relating to individuals on my resentment list—fear of telling someone something that should be said, fear of following through on a particular decision that might affect others, fear of political conflict or social or economic or geographic disasters. I've put down all kinds of fears. I simply listed them, nothing more.

That's *column one.* I fill out all of column one before I go on to column two.

Column Two:

Then the Big Book says "We asked ourselves why we had them." (page 68) So I asked myself why I had each fear. I did this in point form. It was fascinating and instructive. To figure out WHY I had a particular fear meant I had to analyze it.

That's *column two.* I fill out all of column two before I go on to column three.

Why have I been afraid of death, for instance? Not simply because of annihilation, but also because of concern for those I'm leaving behind, concern about pain before death, concern about the unknown, curiosity for what will happen afterwards. Each one of these things tells me a great deal about myself.

If I have to tell a friend something that I don't want to tell but feel that I should, my fear is not simply that I will lose a friend, but they're also that I may be wrong, that my friend will suffer, that I'll be misunderstood, that others may hate me.

If I worry about my daughter's future, my fear is not simply that she won't be happy, but (as I'm honest with myself) that I may feel forced to support her, that I won't have grandchildren, that her fate may somehow make me look like a bad parent.

So the more honest I am in the analysis, the more I discover that some of my reasons for fear are quite understandable, and some are quite self-seeking and selfish, and some are simply stupid! This is in itself a learning experience.

Columns Three and Four:

But the Big Book has more instructions.

It asks us to acknowledge that "self-reliance failed us" and that "we are now on a different basis; the basis of trusting and relying upon God." (page 68)

The form does this by setting out two questions.

Column three is whether we were placing our trust and reliance upon infinite God or our finite selves. Hmmmm. I wonder what the answer to that is going to be? We put a checkmark under "My finite self" for each of the fears we have. I fill out column three for each of my fears before going on to column four.

Column four is whether relying on ourselves worked. Hmmmm. Wonder what that answer is too? Of course it didn't work. If it did work, I wouldn't have these fears! We put a checkmark under "No" for each of the fears we have. I fill out column four for each of the fears before going on to column five.

Column Five:

Now comes *column five.* The Big Book says: "We ask Him to remove our fear and direct our attention to what He would have us be." Here is the simple prayer, and column four just provides us with a box to check that we've said it: "God, please remove my fear of _______, and direct my attention to what you would have me be."

Column Six:

And *column six* requires us to put down what we think that God would have us be. This requires some meditation, and the meditation will yield great rewards!

This is a brilliant prayer. Note it's not "what you would have me do", but "what you would have me be". Here we are getting an insight into ourselves. It's not a question of *action* (what God would have me *do*); it's almost always a matter of *attitude* (what God would have me *be*) which may or may not result in action.

The answer is very often "to be the best I can be under the circumstances"—to be the best father, to be the best friend, maybe even simply to BE rather than to worry or spend my time thinking about useless fears. Or it could be as simple as "to be a person who doesn't worry about these things"!

Whatever it turns out to be, you get a real sense of purpose and direction, which in turn relieves you of fear. And that is the promise we're given at page 68: "At once, we commence to outgrow fear."

Overview:

Fear destroys and paralyzes us and keeps us from being the best we can be. Concentrating on and saying the prayer shows us the nature of an amends to be made by helping us focus on the future in the most constructive, rather than destructive way.

We have been able through this form to separate the reasonable fears from the silly ones. This in itself provides the springboard for removing even the reasonable fears. We REPLACE those fears with acceptance, which is then followed by a sense of direction. Given this reasonable concern, what is the BEST I can make of it? What would my higher power have me be?

If I undertook a risky task, for instance, I would start off with a reasonable fear that I might fall and hurt myself. But that would be accompanied by other unreasonable fears that accompany my fear of hurting myself—for instance that when I fell, my head would hit a jutting out spike and render me completely brain-dead, and my wife and my children would go to ruin taking care of me, and then they would fall into deep depressions and end up committing suicide, and so on and so on. You know what it can be like when we dwell on the worst!

So I would be able to separate the reasonable from the unreasonable fears. In so doing, I would then be in the position, when I prayed to know what my higher power would have me be, in taking my reasonable fear of falling and balancing that against the importance of doing whatever the task might be.

Assuming that it was important to undertake that task, the answer to the question, "What would God have me be?" would be to be a person who takes significant precaution and care, but who resolutely undertakes the task because it must be performed.

On the other hand, my prayer might be answered by a realization that I should be a person who doesn't undertake unimportant tasks that risk my health!

So fears become things we accept and take into account in figuring out what we should be and do.

No wonder the Big Book promises that "at once, we commence to outgrow fear". You will be amazed by how simply this form deals with our fears.

Fear is one of the four character defects isolated by the Resentment Form. We have now outgrown one of our character defects. The Sex Conduct Form will now show us how to live our lives without the other three character defects.

Step Four—Sex Conduct:

If resentments are "the past didn't go my way" and fears are "the future won't go my way", then why does the Big Book discuss Sex Conduct next? I think there's a simple answer.

The true purpose, the Big Book tells us, of the Sex Conduct Inventory is to try "to shape a sane and sound ideal for our future sex life." (page 69)

The purpose of the Sex Conduct Inventory, therefore, is not to deal with our past sex conduct issues. We've dealt with them, if they bother us, under resentments. Nor is its purpose to deal with any sex conduct issues we're worried about in the future. We've dealt with them, if they bother us, under fears.

The purpose of the Sex Conduct Inventory is to figure out how to have a sound relationship right now, in the present, by analyzing out what we did wrong in the past and what we should do in the future, and to deal with the remaining three character defects of selfishness, dishonest, and self-seeking (inconsiderateness) by helping us understand from our past mistakes how we can have relationships that are unselfish, honest, and considerate.

Another key to understanding the Sex Conduct Inventory is to understand the meaning of that phrase. Back in 1939, "sex" did not simply refer to physical sexual activity. It had a broader meaning. It referred to relationships in which there was some physical attraction, but not necessarily the physical activity we now call "sex".

If we look at the most complex relationships we've ever had, we will invariably find that (aside from family) among those relationships were ones in which there was some physical attraction between us and the other person, and the physical attraction was probably unbalanced—one of the two was more attracted than the other. Our physical desires can easily overpower any kind of good thinking, as many of us have experienced.

(Just an aside here. Although we often hear that men generally want physical sex more than women, my experience in talking to so many women in OA is that many OAers—whether men or women—want physical sex more than their significant others. It's an aspect of "wanting everything on the plate", just a general hunger for things. Of course, there are quite significant exceptions to this generalization.)

So if we could figure out what we did wrong in some of our most complex relationships, and know what we should have done, then we have a guide to acting in ALL of our relationships, even with acquaintances or friends. That's why I think the Big Book talks about Sex Conduct. If we've dealt with the past in the Resentment Inventory and the future in the Fear Inventory, it's now time to learn how to live in the present. To live in the present requires us to know how to have real and honest relationships with people. To have real and honest relationships with people, we examine those relationships we've had which were most difficult and learn what to do better in the future.

With that introduction, we go to the instructions in the Big Book, which are all found on page 69. The Big Book points out that "we all have sex problems. We'd hardly be human if we didn't. What can we do about them." Here are the instructions: "We reviewed our own conduct over the years past. Where had we been selfish, dishonest, or inconsiderate? Whom had we hurt?"

Filling out the Sex Conduct Form:

You will see on the form that there is a column for writing down "whom had we hurt", and good advice is simply to fill that *first column* out first. I listed my wife, of course, and many, but not all, of my ex-girlfriends, and a friend I jokingly flirted with, and someone to whom I was strangely attracted but had no real interest in and was very awkward around .

Then the *second column* is where we write where we had been, in relation to the person we put down, "selfish, dishonest, or inconsiderate". Selfish and dishonest retain their meanings, I think, from the resentment inventory—"wanting my way" for selfish and "not telling the truth when the truth should be told, or telling falsehood to others or myself" for dishonest. (Note that we're *starting* where the Resentment form *ended*.) Inconsiderate is simply not thinking of the other person's feelings or interests – being self-seeking.

Then the Big Book asks, "Did we unjustifiably arouse jealousy, suspicion or bitterness?" That's the *third column*, and we fill that out for every person on the list. I find that I don't always check any of those boxes, but I do consider the question carefully each time.

Then the Big Book asks, "Where were we at fault, what should we have done instead?" So that is the *fourth column*—what I should have done instead.

And we fill that out for every person on the list. Patterns immediately emerge. For most of my past relationships, for example, the answer was pretty consistent: I stayed in the relationship longer than was healthy for both me and my ex-girlfriends, and I should have left it earlier on and in a more honest way. For my wife the answer is that I have thought of my own interests, and that I should always love her more and think of her needs more. For the friend I flirted with, I was hurting her and her husband, and I should simply stop flirting with her. For the person I was awkward around, I deprived her of a potential friend.

The Big Book says, "In this way we tried to shape a sane and sound ideal for our future sex life." THAT'S the whole point of this exercise—to know what we did that was wrong, and to know what we should have done instead.

Then the Big Book says, "We subjected each relation to this test—was it selfish or not?" And that's the *fifth column*. Again, selfish has to be looked at in the broad sense that was discussed in Step Three. We check that out for every relationship.

And then we have the Sex Prayer and the Sex Meditation. The Sex Prayer is: "God, please mold my ideals and help me to live up to them." The Sex Meditation is: "God, what should I do about each specific matter." And we say that prayer and that meditation for every person on the list. The Big Book promises us: "The right answer will come, if we want it."

This is a pretty simple form, but it's a very powerful one. We can now extrapolate from our most difficult relationships to all other relationships. We find that our basic approach has to be loving and tolerant and giving; we find that we can't assume too much about other people's intentions or actions; we find, in short, that in some of our most difficult relationships often the greatest barrier has been ourselves.

We have also learned from our mistakes in past relationships how to have relationships without the character defects of selfishness, dishonesty, and self-seeking. Thus we have now dealt with all four character defects through the Fear and Sex Conduct Forms, and we see how we can live our lives without those character defects!

Step Four: Conclusion:

We have now completed our Step Four Inventory from the Big Book's perspective.

It was pretty simple. We filled out some simple forms and learned a lot about ourselves. No matter how many people, institutions, or principles appear on our resentment form; no matter how many fears appear on our fear forms; no matter how many people appear on our sex conduct forms; it doesn't take a very long time to fill them out.

The total amount of writing probably would never exceed 20 hours, and is probably more like 10 hours; but it's probable that you would space those hours out over a few weeks. But if you haven't completed the forms within about six weeks, then either you are incredibly busy with emergency issues (because doing Step Four has to be a major priority—if you don't do it and finish the steps, you will relapse, and to relapse is to die!), or you're procrastinating.

This isn't the place to compare this method of doing Step Four with others; and if you've found a different method that works for you, then there's no reason other than curiosity to try this one. But if doing Step Four has been such a difficult task for you because your current method or your sponsor's method of doing Step Four has you writing for weeks and months and years, then this might be worth trying. I have certainly never found it to be anything less than overwhelming. And it's always short!

The advice of my first sponsor has stayed with me: "Just finish it! It'll never be perfect. So just get this one done so you can recover! After you recover, then you can do more and get more insight.

Note that on page 71 the Big Book suggests that Step Four is simply making "an inventory of your GROSSER handicaps". Now grosser in this context doesn't mean "ewwww"; it simply means "cruder" or "bigger". Step Four is about identifying the BIG character defects. Refining things comes later on, in Step Ten, after we have recovered.

So just get the form done! If necessary, make an appointment to do Step Five just to give you the impetus to finish Step Four.

The Step Four promises:

The Big Book gives us promises on page 70. They're not overwhelming ones, but they do serve as a checklist for us to see if we have done a good Step Four:

> If we have been thorough about our personal inventory, we have written down a lot. We have listed and analyzed our resentments. We have begun to comprehend their futility and their fatality. We have commenced to see their terrible destructiveness. We have begun to learn tolerance, patience and good will toward all men, even our enemies, for we look on them as sick people. We have listed the people we have hurt by our conduct, and are willing to straighten out the past if we can.

Questions:

Now some questions:

- Do your fears prevent you from thinking clearly?
- Do your fears sometimes get you into more trouble rather than less?
- Take an example of a fear that appears to be reasonable (fear of wandering around in a dangerous part of town, for instance) and set out the reasons you have that fear. Did any of your reasons for having that fear turn out to be unreasonable or self-serving?
- Take an example of a fear that appears to be unreasonable (sudden illness of a cautious healthy loved one, for instance) and set out the reasons you have that fear. Did any of your reasons for having that fear turn out to be reasonable?
- What would your higher power have you be in relation to those two fears?
- Have your most difficult relationships been those in which there has been an imbalance of physical attraction?
- Have any of those relationships affected your ability to have relationships with other people even when there has been no issue of physical attraction?
- Take an example of such a relationship and set where you were selfish, dishonest, and inconsiderate.
- What should you have done instead?

Steps Five, Six, and Seven in one day!

You may ask how we can discuss three steps in one chapter? The reason is that the Big Book actually has us do Steps Five, Six, Seven, and even Eight, on the same day.

If you look at the history of the Twelve Steps, you will find that before the Big Book was written there were only six steps—the equivalents of Steps One, Four, Five, Nine, Eleven, and Twelve. Naturally the six steps were handed down from one AAer to another, and there were a lot of unspoken parts to each of the steps. Bill Wilson added the other six steps because the Big Book was going to be read by people who had no one from AA to help them through the steps, and he wanted to make certain that there were no loopholes. So Steps Two, Three, Six, Seven, Eight, and Ten, were added. But the essence of the steps was contained in the original six steps. (You can see this from page 263 of the 4th edition [292 3rd edition], and from the AA publications *AA Comes of Age* and *Pass It On*. I also discuss it in more detail in the Chapter on Step Three.)

We're used to spending a great deal of time and effort thinking about Steps Six and Seven because we read the steps as being equal and we have two major pieces of literature—the OA 12 & 12 and the AA 12 & 12 giving equal number of pages to each step. And if doing that works for you, then I do not suggest making any changes.

I have, however, met many people who have bogged down at Step Six because they don't feel that they are really really ready to have a particular character defect removed, and/or have bogged down at Step Seven because they keep waiting for their character defects to be removed BEFORE they go on to Steps Eight and Nine.

The Big Book's approach is clearly different, and I recommend it to you if you're having trouble doing the steps using other methods, or if you just want a quick and powerful way of recovering form compulsive eating.

The Big Book's approach is very simple. In Steps Four and Five we identify the character defects that block us from our higher power. In Steps Six and Seven we acknowledge our readiness to have those defects removed. And the defects *are* removed through the actions taken in Steps Eight and Nine.

I'll be discussing Steps Eight and Nine together since they go best together.

Step Five:

The Big Book discusses Step Five from pages 71 to 75.

Why?

Pages 71 and 72 are taken up with discussing WHY we have to do Step Five.

The answer is ultimately pretty simple: "If we skip this vital step, we may not overcome drinking [compulsive eating]." (page 72) The Big Book explains this in some detail. It is important, it says, in completing our housecleaning. If, as we found in Steps Three and Four, our problem is one of ego, of self-will, then we have to learn humility—that we aren't and can't be in charge of our own life, let alone the world. People, they say, who don't do Step Five, "had not learned enough of humility, fearlessness and honesty, in the sense we find it necessary, until they told someone else ALL their life story." (page 73) We live, they say, a double life in which we pretend to be someone we're not. "We must be entirely honest with somebody if we expect to live long or happily in this world." (pages 73-74) Page 74 deals with choosing the person we will share our story with.

Aside from the very basic notion of "confession is good for the soul", there are other good reasons as well, not listed in the Big Book. We find that we aren't alone—that the person with whom we're sharing understands us and can probably match every one of our actions with one of his or her own. And we also get insight and feedback that might help us understand ourselves—neither taking ourselves too lightly or too seriously.

Who?

We must remember that the Big Book was published when there were no more than one hundred AAers in the entire world, so the Big Book tells us how to find someone. Later on, in the chapter Working With Others, the Big Book tells us that once we have recovered, we can sponsor people and be the person with whom they do a Step Five (see page 96).

The criteria are simple: "It is important that he be able to keep a confidence; that he fully understand and approve what we are driving at; that he will not try to change our plan" (pages 74-75).

I have found that doing my Step Five with an OAer has been tremendously powerful. OAers understand me. Not only do they fulfill the above criteria, but they also perform another important function: they are able to say, "I'm just like you." Not only have I learned humility, but I have found out that I am not alone. OAers or other Twelve-Steppers can give us that extra ingredient which is so helpful for us isolated and self-pitying selves.

How?

The Big Book then gives us instructions for meeting with the person to whom we tell our story: "We explain to our partner what we are about to do and why we have to do it. He should realize that we are engaged upon a life-and-death errand. Most people approached in this way will be glad to help; they will be honored by our confidence." (page 75) When I do Step Five, I tell my friend how important it is that I do this step, how serious I am about the process.

The Big Book's instructions on actually DOING the step are not very detailed. Here they are: "We pocket our pride and go to it, illuminating every twist of character, every dark cranny of the past" (page 75). That's it. Exactly what are we supposed to do?

I can only give you my experience, based on the nature of our Step Four done the Big Book way, and using the forms which are available at the web site above. I have found this way to be extremely powerful and—added bonus!—quite efficient and relatively brief.

I take the Step Four Resentment form as folded over, with the name of the person, institution, or principle (column one), across from where I have been selfish, dishonest, self-seeking, and frightened (column four).

I read off the name, perhaps give a short identifier or explanation of the name, and then read off what I have written in the fourth column. I invite my friend to probe my responses, to see if there are other things I might write down and didn't think of. I go from name to name.

What I find is that after a few sheets it gets pretty repetitious. I see how my selfishness, my dishonesty, my self-seeking, and my fear, have permeated my entire life, and how I have created virtually identical patterns in so many different situations, and so many different people. I am able, at times to say, "Well, these next three people on the list are exactly the same, so I can take them all together."

Note that we spend no time in talking about the wrongs that others have done to us. This is NOT an opportunity for venting. We are working on what's wrong with us. We might identify some wrongs the others have done in brief in order to assist the person listening to our Step Five to give us some feedback, but if we spend too much time identifying those wrongs, then aren't we really taking the inventory of the other people and not of ourselves?

Then I take the Step Four Fear form and read it across the columns. "Here is one fear [column one], here are the reasons I have it [column two], I placed my trust and reliance upon my finite self [column three] and it didn't work [column four], and I said the Fear Prayer [column five]." I then discuss briefly exactly what I think my higher power would have me be in relation to that fear.

Then I take the Step Four Sex Conduct form and read it across the columns. "Here is a person I hurt [column one], here are the ways in which I was selfish, dishonest, and inconsiderate [column two], I aroused suspicion, but not bitterness or jealousy [column three], what I should have done instead was __________ [column four], the relationship was selfish [column five], and I said the sex prayer [column six] and the sex meditation [column seven]."

Although this may seem mechanical, in fact it is not. With my friend listening and thinking with me about what I might have missed out and telling me that he or she is very similar to me, I feel as if my innermost self has been revealed.

But you can see how little time it need take. I'm not telling my life story from womb to today. I'm not answering a bunch of questions in enormous details. I'm not detailing the wrongs that others have done to me. I'm focusing on my major defects of character and sharing them with another human being.

Promises!

The Big Book makes certain promises at the end of this part of Step Five. If we do not feel these promises, then we have almost certainly left something out, either in Step Four or in Step Five. Here are the promises as found on page 75:

> Once we have taken this step, withholding nothing, we are delighted. We

> can look the world in the eye. We can be alone at perfect peace and ease. Our fears fall from us. We begin to feel the nearness of our Creator. We may have had certain spiritual beliefs, but now we begin to have a spiritual experience. The feeling that the drink problem has disappeared will often come strongly. We feel we are on the Broad Highway, walking hand in hand with the Spirit of the Universe.

In point form:

- Are we delighted?
- Can we look the world in the eye?
- Can we be alone in perfect peace and ease?
- Have we begun to feel the nearness of our Creator?
- Have we begun to have a spiritual experience?
- Although not promised, perhaps we're feeling that the drink problem has disappeared.
- Do we feel we are on the Broad Highway, walking hand in hand with the Spirit of the Universe?

The first time I did this part of Step Five these promises did not come to me. My sponsor suggested I redo Step Four and then do another Step Five. I did that, and the promises still didn't come to me, so I did another Step Four and another Step Five, and then another.

The amazing thing was that each time I "redid" Step Four I discovered new resentments and new fears (and occasionally new sex conduct issues), so I could tell I was going deeper.

After the fourth Step Four and the fourth Step Five these promises came true. It was an amazing experience.

Not yet finished!

But Step Five isn't yet finished. We've admitted to ourselves and another human being the exact nature of our wrongs, but we haven't yet admitted them to God. The Big Book tells us to go home and "find a place where we can be quiet for an hour, carefully reviewing what we have done. We thank God from the bottom of our heart that we know Him better" (page 75). So we review what we've written—we look at all our filled-out forms again. Then we have a prayer: "God, thank you from the bottom of my heart that I know you better." Then the Big Book tells us to study the first five steps and ask our higher power "if we have omitted anything" (page 75). Have we done what has to be done? Have we said what has to be said?

If the answer is yes, and it will probably be yes, then we go on to Step Six that same day. If the answer is no, then we go back and figure out what we left out in either Step Four or Step Five.

The cover of the March 1, 1941 issue of *The Saturday Evening Post* which brought enormous publicity to AA.

Step Six:

Doing Step Four and Five the Big Book way, we have realized that we have four major character defects, all stemming from our wish to have our own way.

- We are selfish—we basically want our way, whether for good or bad or a mixture of reasons.
- We are dishonest—we don't tell others or ourselves the truth about reality.
- We are self-seeking—how others react to us defines how we feel about ourselves and we think of ourselves and not others.
- And we are full of fear.

Out of these four major character defects we have constructed any number of *behaviors* that create problems for us—a tendency to isolate, or to gossip, or to live in a fantasy world, or to manipulate others, or to have bad relationships with others, or to be full of anger, or to be paralyzed by fear, or to be full of lust or gluttony or pride or sloth or greed or envy, or to feel exceedingly sorry for ourselves—or a combination of many of these! But all of these behaviors come down to the four character defects.

Are we ready to have our higher power remove these four major character defects? My experience tells me that you will be if you do Step Four the Big Book way. You won't want to hold on to selfishness, dishonesty, self-seeking, and fear, when you realize how they have truly harmed your life.

Again, it's not the purpose of these essays to compare the Big Book method of doing Step Four with others, but there is a tremendous advantage in understanding these four major character defects rather than thinking that you have 40 major character defects. You're much more willing to give up four huge ones than 40 of varying significance!

> Many inventory methods will list things like "gossip" or "lust" or "gluttony" or "cheating" or "lying" as defects of character. These things appear to me to be *actions*, not defects. A defect of character is something that gives rise to wrong actions.
>
> That's why I like the Big Book's approach to Step Four. I have certainly gossiped. But in and of itself gossiping was not my character defect. I did it because I was selfish, dishonest, self-seeking, and frightened.

The Big Book promises NOTHING at Step Six. Our higher power is not going to remove our character defects at Step Six. The promise of that will only come halfway through Step Nine.

So if you're ready to have your higher power remove these four major character defects, you're on to Step Seven! (If you're not, you say, "God, please help me be willing to remove my character defect of ____________" (page 76). Then go on to Step Seven anyway! Why wait? Recovery is just around the corner.)

Step Seven:

You say the prayer on page 76 of the Big Book.

> My Creator, I am now willing that you should have all of me, good and bad. I pray that you now remove from me every single defect of character which stands in the way of my usefulness to you and my fellows. Grant me strength, as I go out from here, to do your bidding. Amen.

A brilliant prayer. We get to keep some of the minor symptoms of those defects of character which DO NOT stand in the way of our usefulness to our higher power and our fellows. We may have those (I have many of them – interests that occasionally turn into obsessions, for instance).

But it's simply a prayer. The Big Book is very clear about this. There are NO promises for Step Seven either. You just say the prayer and then you're ready for some action!

Overview:

Steps Six and Seven are simply way-stations on these steps. They are moments in time, right after our Step Five, when we consider where we have come from and where we are going to. The removal

> Many OAers, of course, spend much more time on Steps Six and Seven, and recover very powerfully. Some have found the discussions in the AA 12 and 12, or the OA 12 and 12, to be very helpful.
>
> It's not the purpose of this book to argue one way or the other. It's clear, however, that the Big Book's approach is that Steps Six and Seven are done relatively quickly. If you experience relapse while spending time on Steps Six and Seven, maybe you should try to do them as quickly as the Big Book suggests.

of our defects of character comes only when we take action.

The Big Book says: "Now we need more action, without which we find that 'Faith without works is dead.'" Then it talks about Steps Eight and Nine, which we'll talk about next chapter.

Questions for Steps Five, Six, and Seven:

Some questions:

- Do you recognize the importance of sharing your character defects with another human being? Why is it important to you?
- What do you expect from the person who is going to hear your Step Five?
- Will you be open to that person's asking you questions, providing you with feed-back?
- What do you think about the proposition that the behaviors that many of us have understood to be "character defects" (the Seven Deadly Sins, gossiping, etc.) are really symptoms of the four major character defects?
- Can you take something you thought to be a character defect and relate it to the four character defects (selfishness, dishonesty, self-seeking, and fear) discussed by the Big Book?
- Does doing Steps Six and Seven the same day as you do Step Five bother you?
- Why does it bother you? Is it simply because you think you should spend as much time on those steps as all the others? Because you've been told you should? Or because you think something may be missing? If so, what?

The Big Book suggests that we do Step Eight the same day that we do Steps Five, Six, and Seven. But we'll discuss Steps Eight and Nine together in the next chapter.

Dr. Bob Smith

Steps Eight and Nine:

Steps Eight and Nine are not discussed separately in the Big Book. They discuss one action—making amends—which is broken down into two parts—being ready to make amends to everyone we've hurt, and only making amends if we won't hurt other people, including those we've already hurt.

These are the action steps which actually bring us recovery from compulsive eating. They are the steps which remove our character defects and allow us to become different people—recovered people, people full of hope who are able to transmit that hope to the compulsive eater who still suffers.

The Big Book's instructions are simple. First we make a list of people we had harmed and figure out what harm we've done them. We made that list, the Big Book says, "when we took inventory" (page 76). Then we make those amends unless to do so would injure them or others. Really quite simple.

Types of Amends:

What kinds of amends are there?

<u>Direct Amends:</u>

The Big Book—through examples—lists three kinds of direct amends.

- The first is **eyeball to eyeball**—"I am sorry for what I have done."
- The second is **restitution**—"I will make up for what I have done."
- The third is **taking the public consequences**—"I will make known to other people what I have done."

Each of these is discussed by detailed example twice—the first time to describe the nature of the amends and the second time to discuss how to deal with situations in which others might be hurt by making that amends.

The first amends—*eyeball to eyeball*—is described from the bottom of page 76 to the middle of page 78 with the example of confronting a person face to face and apologizing for our side of the action. That same amends is then described from the harm-to-others perspective from the bottom of page 80 to the middle of page 82 with the example of whether or not to tell a spouse of an extra-marital affair.

The second amends—*restitution*—is described on page 78 with the example of debts; and then described from the harm-to-others perspective on page 79 with the example of paying alimony to an ex-wife with the result of harming the current family.

The third amends — *public consequences* — is described from the bottom of page 78 to the top of page 79 with the example of willingness to go to jail; and then described from the harm-to-others perspective on page 80 with the example of making up for a lost reputation.

When you think about it, these are the only three kinds of direct amends. You go directly to a person and apologize and/or make up for the harm you've done; or if the harm you've done has had broader consequences, you have to make broader amends.

<u>Living Amends:</u>

The Big Book discusses living amends from the middle of page 82 to the middle of page 83. Here the concept is that direct amends simply aren't enough for people with whom we have had long-term relationships; they don't need apologies or restitution—they need a new person to have a relationship with.

<u>Amends we cannot make:</u>

And on page 83 the Big Book discusses amends we can't make, and promises us that if we are ready to make them, that is good enough.

The Big Book provides two basic rules for making amends. The first is that if they are possible to make, we must make them or else we will not recover. The second is that in making our amends, we sweep our side of the street off and don't deal with the wrongs others have done to us. (I'll deal with variants of that issue a little later in this chapter.)

Filling in the Form for Steps Eight and Nine

The Steps Eight and Nine Form available on the web site and following this chapter is pretty self-explanatory.

First you write down the names of persons (and institutions) you have harmed.

Second you figure out what harm you've done them.

Third, using the three kinds of direct amends and living amends as a guide, you work out what kind of amends you could possibly make to make up for the harm done.

Fourth, you ask yourself whether making those kinds of amends would injure other people, including the person you've harmed. If the answer is yes, you don't make the amend; but perhaps you can think of alternative amends that might be made that could at least mend some harm. If the answer is no, that making those amends would not harm others, then you should make the amend.

Although not in the Big Book, the form also contains those well-known OA/AA columns of "Now, Sometimes, Never", so you can figure out a priority for making the various amends you have to make. If you do the amends in the "Now" column, you will find it so fulfilling that the amends in the "sometimes" column end up in the "now" column and the amends in the "never" column end up in the "sometimes" column. And so on. That's the experience of those who have made amends. Although they seem to be scary, they are ultimately overwhelmingly satisfying. The more amends you make, the more you want to finish them, because you feel much closer to your higher power than ever.

Simple amends are those that are very clear, just like the Big Book examples. You lied to someone—you apologize. You stole money or caused economic hardship—you pay it back. You harmed a person's reputation—you restore the person's reputation.

The complex amends:

What about the difficult ones?

Let's take a common area of concern for many OAers I have met—the person who has in fact been very badly dealt with by another person—perhaps sexually or physically abused or, less intensely, betrayed. What have our Steps Four and Five taught us about any harms we have done to that person?

Remember that our own character defects are selfishness, dishonesty, self-seeking, and fear. Have those character defects harmed the person who has harmed us; and if so, how?

If you recall our discussion of Step Four, one fact that we faced is that the more a person has harmed others, the more that person has become less capable of being a human being.

Remember that we prayed for that person to have what we wanted out of life—and when we prayed for that person to have serenity, to be able to love and to be loved, to have good relationships, to feel at peace, we knew suddenly that that person could have none of those things because that person had done horrible harm to us and perhaps others.

So what harm have we done to them?

At the very least, we expected them to change, we hoped for them to change, we thought they were capable of being more than they were.

An amends for that is to stop having high expectations of them, to stop thinking that they could change, to treat them with pity and compassion, NOT to let them continue harming us by our trying to re-create history, and NOT continuing to feel fear and guilt about what occurred. They should not be able to continue to harm us!

And then there's another possible aspect.

For many of these people, we were silent when we should have been speaking the truth. We should have stopped what they were doing BEFORE it got worse. (Of course we realize this looking back. We don't blame ourselves for what we did or didn't do at an earlier time. We are looking to see what we COULD have done so we can make sure that things like that don't happen in the future.)

So a possible amends might be an apology for not having stopped them in time. It might also be stopping that person from doing harm to others by going public.

I have a friend who found it necessary to tell her relatives who had children about the sexual abuse she suffered from a relative who was still around and still spending time with the children of those relatives; she felt that was the least she could to try to prevent that person from doing harm to himself or others.

On the other side, I have a friend whose amends to her sexual abuser was to let him alone—he was old and decrepit and was, in her eyes, pitiful. He could do no more harm to himself or to others.

So we have to think about whether or not going public in some way would cause more or less harm for that person. It's a question of balance. If we wanted to stop a child from stepping off a cliff, it might be necessary to grab his/her arm in a way that could cause a broken arm.

Amends we can't make:

There are amends, though, that we can't make because they would directly harm other people.

Our OA 12 & 12 gives a great example—something like, "Hello, Mom? Listen, I hated you for 20 years and I just want to apologize for that. I love you now." There's an example of an amends that would hurt, not help, the person to whom it is made. It's similar to the Big Book's example of not telling a spouse of an extra-marital affair if the spouse doesn't know about it.

There are many such situations. In my own life, there are some ex-girlfriends from many years ago to whom I would like to apologize. But what right do I have to enter into their lives now, after not having spoken to them for that length of time? Or to remind them of something they might have forgotten? Might it not be harmful to them? What right do I have to do something for my own benefit that might harm them?

I have consulted with sponsors over the years, and have concluded that it would be selfish of me to speak to them out of the blue in that way. If I'm ever in a city where one of them lives, I might phone and see if she wanted to go for coffee and then perhaps get a feel for whether or not it might not be harmful to apologize. But the fact that I'm ready today to apologize makes me clean—I'm not the kind of person now who would do what I did so many years ago!

Or another example: I used to gossip about a particular person, making fun of his/her foibles. Through Step 4 and 5 I realized how selfish, dishonest, self-seeking, and frightened I was in relation to that person. The direct amends that could be made is to say, "Look, I told true stories about you that have held you up to ridicule among your peers. I'm sorry. I won't do it again." But that person doesn't know I gossiped about him/her.

I've decided, again after consulting with sponsors over the years, that it would be harmful to apologize. But what I do do is no longer gossip about him or anyone else, and if I'm in a situation where people gossip about him/her, I say something like, "I used to gossip about him/her, but I no longer do, because I think that kind of gossip makes fun of someone who is not well and I don't think it's right to make fun of people who are not well."

Those are examples of amends we could make but shouldn't make.

What about amends we *can't* make—people who are dead, for instance? There are many suggestions, of course, ranging from just being serene because we know we're ready to make amends, to having imaginary conversations with them, to doing symbolic things like writing them letters and scattering the pieces to the winds or going to their gravestones. What works for one person may not work for another.

Living Amends:

Living amends are just that. It is not sufficient for me to say to my wife or my children, "Oops, I wasn't such a good husband or father. Sorry." I have to BECOME a better husband and a better father. This requires working through those areas where I was not a good husband and father and making certain that I'm doing what I should be doing. I've been working on this a long time, of course. I'm not a perfect husband or father, and I don't always know what the right course of action is. But I've learned to do more things around the house, to think more of others, and I hope that I've been able to show—not to say, but to show—that I'm a better person than I was.

Step Eight Prayers:

The Big Book gives us Step Eight prayers.

If we're not willing to go to others and make amends, the Big Book suggests on page 76 : "If we haven't the will to do this, we ask until it comes."

And on page 79:

> Reminding ourselves that we have decided to go to any lengths to find a spiritual experience, we ask that we be given strength and direction to do the right thing, no matter what the personal consequences may be. We may lose our position or reputation or face jail, but we are willing. We have to be. We must not shrink at anything.

So our prayers are clear: "God, give me the will to do this. God, please give me the strength and direction to do the right thing, no matter what the personal consequences may be."

The questions will be asking you to give examples of working out difficult issues and figuring out what the amends should be for other people's benefits.

One thing I know for certain.

If we have done Steps Four, Five, Six, Seven, to the best of our abilities, and have worked out the harms we have done and are ready to make the amends for those harms, then our motives will be as pure as they can be, and what we say or do for the other person will BE the right thing to say or do.

And I believe the reverse is true—that if our motives are not pure, if we think of ourselves and hope that if we make amends the other person will apologize for what he or she did, that we'll get that promotion, that we'll get credit for doing the right thing—then what we say or do will NOT be the right thing to say or do. It is a matter of the right attitude.

The Big Book tells us, at page 83, what our attitude must be:

> We should be sensible, tactful, considerate and humble without being servile or scraping. As God's people we stand on our feet; we don't crawl before anyone.

Now that attitude comes from one major spot. It is that we are trying to be rid of the things in ourselves, our defects of character, which block us from our higher power, and we realize that without making amends it will be impossible for our defects to be removed. We won't be removing them—that's the miracle from our higher power—but we will be taking the actions necessary to have them removed.

When we realize this, making amends becomes a matter of extreme urgency. Remember that until we do this, we are not freed from the foods we know cause our cravings. We may have temporary release, but it cannot constitute the recovery we're seeking until we have begun working these steps.

More than that, we see that having those defects of character removed by making the amends means that we are becoming entirely DIFFERENT people from who we were. We are NOT the people who did the things we are making amends for. We can be reborn. That is why we stand on our feet and don't crawl before anyone. "Yes, I used to be like that, but, God willing, I am no longer like that." What peace that brings!

An example of false humility:

In a small town in Russia in the late 1800s, in a small synagogue, the congregation is praying to God during Yom Kippur—the highest of all holy days.

The rabbi gets up and says, "God, before You I am nothing, I am nothing," and falls onto the floor.

The richest man in town gets up and says, "God, before You I am nothing, I am nothing," and falls onto the floor.

The town beggar gets up and says, "God, before You I am nothing, I am nothing," and falls onto the floor.

The rich man whispers to the rabbi: "Look who thinks *he's* nothing!"

Amends to myself?

Note, by the way, that neither the Big Book nor the steps themselves ever talks about making amends to ourselves, which is often said in OA meetings. The only amends we make to ourselves is to have our higher power remove those character defects which stand in the way of our usefulness to our higher power and to our fellows. That's the "only" amends—but it's a huge one. To have those character defects removed is to place us in direct relationship with our higher power. There is no greater amends.

We often hear people talk about "the biggest amends I have to make is to myself". But that really comes down to people saying, "I have to learn to say 'no'" or "I can't run myself ragged without taking time for myself"—quite commendable concepts. But if you look at the Big Book approach, which is to focus on others rather than ourselves, you will see how this concept of an "amends to myself" is consistent with what's been discussed above.

Of course we have to learn to be honest and to say no, because many of us have been enablers and people-pleasers who have said yes for the wrong reasons and have thereby allowed other people to harm us, others, AND themselves. If we make amends to them by not being enablers and not being people-pleasers, we've said "no" but we've said it for the right reasons—to help others, not to be nice to ourselves. And if we run ourselves ragged, then what use are we to the compulsive eater who still suffers?

Of course we have to take care of ourselves; we are messengers of the greatest message in the world—recovery through the Twelve Steps. So we have to take care of ourselves to make certain that others can hear that message.

But the FOCUS is on helping others and making amends to others, and not on ourselves.

The Promises:

And the Big Book FINALLY gives us really good promises. We haven't had great ones up to now (Step Three—an effect will be felt; Step Four—we have learned about our character defects; Step Five—some better ones—we will feel at peace and ease; none for Steps Six and Seven). Halfway through Step Nine come the Promises (page 83), which many of us know well. (By the way, people keep trying to find Twelve Promises. There are three different ways of finding them. I'm giving my favorite way.)

> If we are painstaking about this phase of our development, we will be amazed before we are half way through.
>
> [1] We are going to know a new freedom and a new happiness.
>
> [2] We will not regret the past nor wish to shut the door on it.
>
> [3] We will comprehend the word serenity and we will know peace.
>
> [4] No matter how far down the scale we have gone, we will see how our experience can benefit others.
>
> [5] That feeling of uselessness and self-pity will disappear.
>
> [6] We will lose interest in selfish things and gain interest in our fellows.
>
> [7] Self-seeking will slip away.
>
> [8] Our whole attitude and outlook upon life will change.
>
> [9] Fear of people and of economic insecurity will leave us.
>
> [10] We will intuitively know how to handle situations which used to baffle us.
>
> [11] We will suddenly realize that God is doing for us what we could not do for ourselves.
>
> Are these extravagant promises? We think not. They are being fulfilled among us—sometimes quickly, sometimes slowly.
>
> [12] They will always materialize if we work for them.

These are true promises! Look how they promise nothing about our environment or our financial situation or anything practical. What they basically say is that we have had a spiritual awakening that has made us into different people; we are now able to learn from the past instead of dwelling on it in misery; and we can live in the present with serenity and love. It is precisely the promise of the Appendix on Spiritual Experience: we have had "a profound alteration" in our "attitude to life." What marvelous promises they are! And they do come true.

The "Hidden" Promises:

Now, with the promise of a spiritual awakening halfway through Step Nine comes the fulfillment of the promise made to the compulsive eater in Step Two—that the miracle will happen and our trigger foods and eating behaviors will no longer tempt us. Here are the Hidden Promises, found on pages 84 and 85:

> And we have ceased fighting anything or anyone - even alcohol. For by this time sanity will have returned. We will seldom be interested in liquor. If tempted, we recoil from it as from a hot flame. We react sanely and normally, and we will find that this has happened automatically. We will see that our new attitude toward liquor has been given us without any thought or effort on our part. It just comes! That is the miracle of it. We are not fighting it, neither are we avoiding temptation. We feel as though we had been placed in a position of neutrality - safe and protected. We have not even sworn off. Instead, the problem has been removed. It does not exist for us. We are neither cocky nor are we afraid. That is our experience.

This is what we've been waiting for! This is why we joined OA in the first place. The mental obsession/insanity has been released from us. We're finally sane!

I recently ate one of the most memorable meals of my life. Every single piece of every single dish was cooked to perfection. I actually savored each bite of the asparagus spears and the baby carrots served with the entree. I put my fork down between bites. Simple but exquisite tastes filled my mouth.

It's not hard to compare this experience with what eating used to be like before I achieved this sanity. Sure, my first bite might have given me the same kind of pleasure as my first bite of the asparagus spear. But the rest of my eating was an attempt to recapture the initial pleasure. There was a kind of desperation to my eating. My cravings forced me to continue eating until nothing was left, even if I never recaptured the initial pleasure.

No, eating before I finished Step Nine was not a happy experience!

Conclusion:

Done the Big Book way, this has taken us only a few weeks or months. We've pushed on from Steps Five through Nine quickly, and we have got our relief before our mental obsession overcame us and we returned to our trigger foods and eating behaviors; and now we're released from that mental obsession so we are protected. This is great joy! Those are REAL amends to ourselves!

Questions:

Here are some questions:

- For those of you who have made amends, what were your greatest worries before you made those amends, and did any of those things matter after you made them?
- If you have been silent about harms done to you, do you see how that silence has harmed those who did harm to you? And if so, will relieving that silence help those who did harm or not?
- Are there, or have there been, amends you felt compelled to make which potentially placed others at risk of harm, but which you felt overall were better to do for their sake than not to do?
- For those of you have done your amends, have the Promises and the Hidden Promises come true for you? Describe it.

The Hidden Promises come true but the Big Book cautions us on page 85: "That is how we react SO LONG as we keep in fit spiritual condition."

In the next chapter, therefore, we'll study the first and the second of the three steps that keep us in fit spiritual condition—Steps Ten and Eleven.

The next page is a simple form for Steps Eight and Nine.

A replica of the church directory which Bill Wilson looked at in the Mayflower Hotel on May 11, 1935.

At www.oabigbook.info you can download the Step 8 & 9 form and fill it in on your computer using Adobe Reader.

Clear Data

STEP EIGHT AND NINE LIST

This form is not taken in its entirety from the Big Book, but is a useful guide. Fill out the form directly from the saved copies of your Fourth Step Inventory worksheets. Complete all Amends marked in the "Now?" column. When done, move the items from the "Sometime?" column to "Now?" and the "Never!" items to "Sometime?" You'll find that the Nevers have turned into Sometimes, and the Sometimes into Nows. Continue this process until you complete all items on your Ninth Step.

				Ready to do the Amend(s)...		
Name of person harmed:	**Harm done to that person:**	**Possible Amend(s) for that harm (Apology, Restitution, Public Acknowledgement, Living)**	**Will this Amend harm that person or anyone else?**	**Now?**	**Some-time?**	**Never!**
			Yes No	☐	☐	☐
			Yes No	☐	☐	☐
			Yes No	☐	☐	☐
			Yes No	☐	☐	☐
			Yes No	☐	☐	☐
			Yes No	☐	☐	☐

Steps Ten and Eleven—Introduction:

We ended our discussion of Step Nine with the Hidden Promises of pages 84 and 85. The Big Book ends those promises with a very clear warning: "That is how we react so long as we keep in fit spiritual condition."

If we do not keep in fit spiritual condition, we will relapse. Our mental obsession will return. We will become insane again.

How do we keep in fit spiritual condition? You might recall Dr. Bob's summary of the Twelve Steps: "Clean House, Trust God, Help Others." We will find that once we have recovered, that summary means Step Ten (Clean House), Step Eleven (Trust God), Step Twelve (Help Others).

Step Ten:

For my first six years in program, I went through a cycle of recovery and relapse, recovery and relapse. This happened until I was finally introduced to the Big Book's approach to recovery. As I began to recover using the Big Book approach, I analyzed what had gone wrong in my first six years. I discovered two things that were the main cause of my relapses.

The *first* was that I had refused to accept that there were certain foods and eating behaviors that caused me uncontrollable cravings—the notion of the "allergy of the body" that I discussed at length in our discussion of Step One. I had fallen prey to the notion that all the diets I had ever been on, and all the "experts" I read, told me, which was that after I lost my weight I could eat ANYTHING in moderation; so I "took back" foods that I had eliminated during my weight-loss time, tried to eat them in moderation; and soon found that I was gorging on them.

The *second*, though, was far more serious: there had been a number of times when I was trying to stay away from my trigger foods but I still found rationalizations to return to them—the "mental obsession" that I also discussed at length in Step One. Why was this mental obsession returning? Why were my "best" efforts not to eat these foods being undermined by my complete lack of will?

I discovered the reason by looking back on how I felt right after I had completed Step Nine each time I went through the steps after my relapses. Right after Step Nine I felt absolutely great. Food wasn't a problem for me. The "hidden promises" were true; I was placed in a position of complete neutrality. Yet that feeling of neutrality, of power over food, dissipated quickly and I went back to it after a few months.

Why was this? I was meditating—had five meditation books and said my prayers. I was sponsoring and giving service galore. So Steps Eleven and Twelve were covered. But how was I doing Step Ten?

Well, I was reading it "on the wall"—"Continued to take personal inventory and when we were wrong promptly admitted it." So as life went on, and I yelled at my kids or began to feel bad about something, I admitted it. I apologized. That's all I did. That's all I thought I should do.

As I began to study the Big Book's approach and learned, with the help of great teaching tapes, to look beyond the steps "on the wall" and read the Big Book's actual instructions, I realized the mistake I had made.

Here are the Big Book's instructions for Step Ten:

> Continue to watch for selfishness, dishonesty, resentment, and fear. When these crop up, we ask God at once to remove them. We discuss them with someone immediately and make amends quickly if we have harmed anyone. Then we resolutely turn our thoughts to someone we can help.

If you look at those instructions, you will see pretty clearly that they are really the equivalent of doing Steps Four, Five, Six, Seven, Eight, and Nine. Here's the annotated version of the same instructions:

> Continue to watch for selfishness, dishonesty, resentment, and fear. [STEP FOUR—In Step Four we encountered the concepts of "selfishness, dishonest, resentment, and fear". Clearly that's what the Big Book is talking about!] When these crop up, we ask God at once to remove them. [STEPS SIX AND SEVEN] We discuss them with someone immediately [STEP FIVE] and make amends quickly if we have harmed anyone. [STEPS EIGHT AND NINE] Then we resolutely turn our thoughts to someone we can help.

So Step Ten is Steps Four through Nine done in the context of recovery. We do exactly what we did in Steps Four through Nine, except we've recovered and we're trying to keep that recovery. When I finished Step Nine, I had dealt with my past, and had no fears for the future.

But each minute and day and week AFTER I finished my Step Nine means a little bit, and then a lot more, PAST that I have to deal with, and the only way I can deal with it is to do what I did successfully before—write it out, share it with another human being, realize my character defects, ask my higher power to remove them, and make amends for any mistakes I have made.

You'll recall that when we discussed Step Four, I pointed out that the complete inventory is really not just Step Four but Steps Four through Nine. Understanding that is the whole point to understanding Step Ten!

I have a simple twelve-point checklist (it just happened to be 12!) for when I do a Step Ten. I look at "The Doctor's Opinion" and find the words "They are restless, irritable and discontented unless they can again experience the sense of ease and comfort which comes at once by taking a few drinks". I look at page 52 in "We Agnostics" and find the Bedevilments: "We were having trouble with personal relationships, we couldn't control our emotional natures, we were a prey to misery and depression, we couldn't make a living, we had a feeling of uselessness, we were full of fear, we were unhappy, we couldn't seem to be of real help to other people". I also look at my food issues.

So my Twelve Step checklist for when I do a Step Ten is:

1. Am I restless? (*Doctor's Opinion*)
2. Am I irritable? (*Doctor's Opinion*)
3. Am I discontented? (*Doctor's Opinion*)
4. Am I having trouble with personal relationships? (Bedevilments)
5. Can I not control my emotional nature? (Bedevilments)
6 Am I a prey to misery and depression? (Bedevilments)
7. Can I not make a living? (Bedevilments)
8. Do I have a feeling of uselessness? (Bedevilments)
9. Am I full of fear? (Bedevilments)
10. Am I unhappy? (Bedevilments)
11. Am I not of real help to other people? (Bedevilments)
12. Is my food or quantity of food getting sloppy?

If the answer to any one or more of these questions is YES, then it's time for me to clean house again.

So I take out my Step Four forms and I fill them out; I do a Step Five, and then a Six and a Seven, and I figure out and then do my amends.

What I usually find is that my amends turn out to be living amends, for the most part. I usually find that something has been going on in my life that is bugging me and I haven't really noticed it or given it much thought. And I get clean again and the answers to all the above twelve questions is a resounding NO and I get the promises again!

I also find, by the way, that when I finish the Step Four part of the Step Ten I've already got most of my insights into what's been bugging me. Step Five provides fewer insights,because I've already become clear about what my defects of character are. But I still do Steps Five and Six and Seven and then make amends quickly. (Often I will grab the last recovered person leaving my regular meeting and just ask for ten minutes of his or her time to do the Step Five part of my Step Ten.) My amends are usually living amends.

As we'll see in the discussion of Step Eleven immediately following, the nighttime meditation also has the equivalent of Steps Four through Nine, so I had to consider what the difference is between a nighttime Step Eleven meditation doing Steps Four through Nine, and a Step Ten doing Steps Four through Nine. They're both done in the context of recovery. We've already had the miracle. How do we keep it?

Here's what I've come down to.

The Step Eleven evening meditation is done at night to review the day you've had. I'll talk more about that in a little while. Step Ten, however, is designed to deal with the resentments, fears, and sex conduct issues that have accumulated since you last did a Step Four through Nine or a Step Ten.

In other words, it's for the big things that you haven't been able to capture during your evening meditations.

So Step Ten isn't as dramatic as Steps Four through Nine, when I'm learning so much about myself and where I'm really cleaning out the past respecting actions I've taken in the past. But Step Ten becomes essential to keep my house clean!

Refining Step Ten:

One thing I've been doing lately with really powerful results is to use the Step Four Resentment form a little differently. For some very significant issues in my life, instead of writing those issues down in column 1, and writing down why those issues are in my mind in column 2, I've been taking what I would normally put down in column 2 and putting each one of those points as a separate point in column 1.

For example, I was trying to make a decision as to whether or not to change my career. In a Step Four I would write down "My career" in column 1, and then some points in column 2 like "I'm bored", "I want to feel more useful", "I'm worried about making money".

What I've been doing lately in Step Ten is putting down as separate resentments each of the ideas I would normally put down as *reasons* in column 2 for the resentments.

For example, instead of putting "my career" down in column 1, instead I'll put down "I'm bored" and "I want to feel more useful" and "I'm worried about making money" into column 1. Then, when I get around to column 2, I ask myself why *these* resentments are on my mind.

This has given me much deeper insight into the issues because I'm going deeper and deeper into my motivations and attitudes to life.

I wouldn't recommend this for Step Four. Step Four is to deal with the big stuff. But I sure do recommend it for major issues that you have to deal with in Step Ten. It clears your thinking!

It's because of this approach to Step Ten that I haven't had a relapse for over thirteen years. When I look at the journeys of people I have sponsored, it is precisely those who have not done Step Ten on a regular basis who have relapsed, unfortunately following the path I walked for my first six years in program!

I urge you—whenever you feel stressed out or kind of icky or food begins to become attractive—to do a Step Ten by repeating Steps Four through Nine!

I call this a Step Ten! It is NOT Steps Four through Nine because those are the steps that BRING us to recovery by allowing our higher power to remove our defects of character and give us sanity.

Now that we have recovered, we keep our sanity and our closeness to our higher power by doing Step Ten.

In Step Ten we Clean House. In Step Eleven we Trust God. In Step Twelve we Help Others. Dr. Bob's prescription for life is our guide!

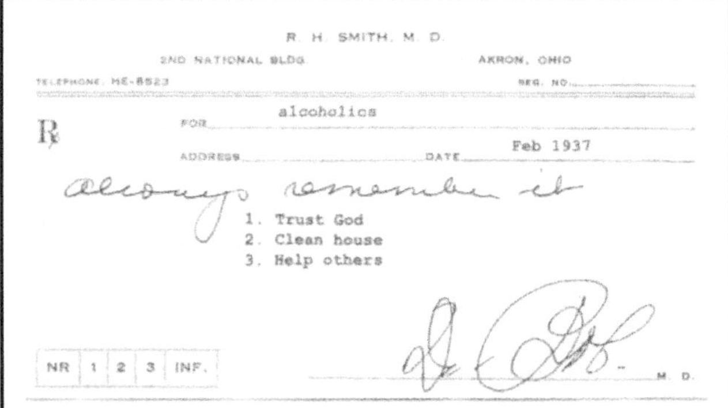

R. H. SMITH, M. D.
2ND NATIONAL BLDG. AKRON, OHIO
TELEPHONE, HE-8523 REG. NO.
℞ FOR alcoholics
ADDRESS DATE Feb 1937
always remember it
1. Trust God
2. Clean house
3. Help others
NR 1 2 3 INF. M. D.

This may or may not be a real "prescription" signed by Dr. Bob. A copy of his prescription pad is available, and someone may very well have created a great fake to circulate on the Web. On the other hand, it may be real, since Dr. Bob often said what's written here. It's great to look at, at any rate!

Step Eleven:

And now Step Eleven. If you have downloaded the Step Eleven form to be found at **www.oabigbook.info**, or look at the form preceding this chapter, you will see how that form provides all specific instructions from pages 86 to 88 (plus a few others), so I'm not going to go over those specific instructions. I just want to point out a few things.

The Big Book's warning about needing to keep in fit spiritual condition begins its discussion of Step Eleven. On page 84:

> It is easy to let up on the spiritual program of action and rest on our laurels. We are headed for trouble if we do, for alcohol is a subtle foe. We are not cured of alcoholism. What we really have is a daily reprieve contingent on the maintenance of our spiritual condition. Every day is a day when we must carry the vision of God's will into all of our activities. 'How can I best serve Thee - Thy will (not mine) be done.' These are thoughts which must go with us constantly. We can exercise our will power along this line all we wish. It is the proper use of the will.

(A "reprieve" is a suspension of a death sentence!)

The Big Book then talks about "receiving strength, inspiration, and direction" from our higher power. The whole concept is to develop a "vital sixth sense" that gives us a direct connection to the power which is greater than we are. We are trying to learn to act intuitively—directly from our hearts with the purest of motives. We have lived, at the very least, a double life; in my case, at times, it was a triple or quadruple life. Now we have to live according to the dictates of our higher power.

Specific Directions:

The Big Book contains specific directions. "It would be easy to be vague about this matter. Yet, we believe we can make some definite and valuable suggestions." (page 86)

These suggestions are, in effect, the MINIMUM we should be doing. I know many people who spend an hour or two meditation in the morning, using any number of powerful meditation techniques. They are very spiritual people, and I respect them tremendously. But at the minimum they also do what the Big Book suggests!

The Big Book has three kinds of prayers and meditations.

The *first* is what we do on going to sleep, as discussed in the first full paragraph on page 86.

The *second* is what we do on awakening, as discussed in the last two paragraphs on page 86, and the first three paragraphs on page 87.

The *third* is what we do during the daytime, discussed in the last paragraph on page 87, going on to page 88.

Why is the nighttime prayer and meditation discussed first? Interestingly enough, the original manuscript had us review the day before when we woke up in the morning, and someone must have pointed out to Bill that it would be far wiser to review the day just when we're going to sleep.

Clearly the intent, whether done before we go to sleep or when we wake up, is to be clear about how we spent the day just passed.

The evening prayer and mediation:

The evening prayer and meditation is really a Step Four through Nine inventory, isn't it? Here's the annotated version:

> Were we resentful, selfish, dishonest or afraid? [STEP FOUR] Do we owe an apology? [STEPS EIGHT AND NINE] Have we kept something to ourselves which should be discussed with another person at once? [STEP FIVE] Were we kind and loving toward all? What could we have done better? Were we thinking of ourselves most of the time? Or were we thinking of what we could do for others, of what we could pack into the stream of life? But we must be careful not to drift into worry, remorse or morbid reflection, for that would diminish our usefulness to others. After making our review we ask God's forgiveness and inquire what corrective measures should be taken. [STEPS SIX AND SEVEN]

Sure, it's not in the same order, but the actions are very similar. As I said in the discussion of Step Ten, I think this Steps Four through Nine is done informally, maybe even in bed, but certainly not necessarily with pen and paper. This is what we do just before we go to sleep.

Note, though, that we don't do a "Step Five" unless we have to—the question is whether we have "kept something to ourselves which should be discussed with another person at once". Maybe we haven't. So there's a difference.

The more carefully we do this, remembering every little thing that happened to us that day and analyzing it, we will probably deal with most of the difficult things in our lives on a day-to-day basis. But I find that doing that doesn't give me the kind of overview I need to look at all the biggest things in my life. I might be irritated day to day by my children and deal with those irritations in my Step Eleven sleep-time prayer and meditation. But ultimately my big issues with my children will almost certainly be dealt with in a Step Ten.

At least that's how I do it. I know that many people who work the steps the Big Book way do their Steps Four through Nine every night by writing and analyzing their day and phoning their sponsors. They have decided that Step Ten is to be done every night, and that the sleep-time prayer and meditation includes a full Step Ten. And it certainly works for them, and those of them I know are really more spiritual than I am, so they probably know more than I do. I just find it more convenient to work it this way. I work what I would call a "good enough" program.

The emphasis on the evening prayer and mediation is to figure out what I could do better for the next day. It is not introspective. We review our past day to see how we did, and how we can do better.

The morning prayer and meditation:

Planning our day ahead on awakening is pretty clear.

We're given wonderful instructions for clearing our mind and thinking through things with the best of motives. The most wonderful and freeing thing is the instruction that if we don't know what we should be doing, if we "face indecision", we pray for "inspiration, an intuitive thought or a decision" and then "we relax and take it easy. We don't struggle." (Page 86) It is truly remarkable what happens when we do it this way. At least that's been my experience, and the experience of countless hundreds of people I've talked to over the years.

In effect, at least from a psychological point of view, we're letting our subconscious take over, and if our subconscious is filled with good motives, then it will do a great job for us! And for those who are more religious, they find that they hear their God's directions very very clearly!

The daytime prayer and meditation:

And the daytime prayers! There are times when I have to repeat "Thy will not mine be done. Thy will not mine be done. Thy will not mine be done." over and over and over again until I calm down and get some sense of direction. But it works!

Following this page is the Step Eleven form, listing all the prayers that the Big Book sets out.

Questions:

Here are some questions:

- If you're not up to Step Ten yet, do you see the correlation between Steps Four through Nine and Step Ten?
- If you've relapsed in the past, is it possible that you failed to continue to clean house by doing Step Ten?
- Do you see a distinction between Step Ten and the sleep-time prayer and meditation?
- How do you feel about the notion of praying for the right thought or action or decision, and then just letting go?
- The Big Book suggests at page 87 that for our awakening prayers "we sometimes select and memorize a few set prayers which emphasize the principles we have been discussing." Aside from the Step Three and Seven prayers, the Serenity Prayer, and the St. Francis Prayer (from Step Eleven in the AA 12 & 12), can you suggest some short prayers "which emphasize the principles we have been discussing"?
- How do you feel about the concept that once you have recovered at Step Nine, you simply maintain your fit spiritual condition through Steps Ten, Eleven, and Twelve. In other words, how do you feel about the notion that, in effect, you don't go through the steps again?

STEP 11 PRAYERS AND MEDITATIONS

Evening Prayer and Meditation

Big Book, page 86;

On retiring at night, constructively review your day:

- Were you resentful, selfish, dishonest or afraid?
- Do you owe an apology?
- Have you kept something to yourself which should be discussed with another person at once?
- Were you kind and loving toward all?
- What could you have done better?
- Were you thinking of yourself most of the time?
- Or were you thinking of what you could do for others, of what you could pack into the stream of life?

Be careful not to drift into worry, remorse or morbid reflection, for that would diminish your usefulness to others.

After making your review:

God, please forgive me and tell me what corrective measures should be taken.

Morning Prayer and Meditation

Big Book, pages 86-7;

On awakening pray:

God, I ask you to direct my thinking, I especially ask that my thinking be divorced from self-pity, dishonest or self-seeking motives.

Think about the twenty-four hours ahead, Consider your plans for the day...

If you are faced with indecision, pray:

I ask you for inspiration, an intuitive thought, or a decision.

After considering your plans for the day, pray:

God, I pray that I be shown all through the day what my next step is to be. I pray that I be given whatever I need to take care of such problems. I ask especially for freedom from self-will. I ask that I be given strength only if others will be helped.

Also say the following prayers:

My creator, I ask that you show me the way of patience, tolerance, kindliness and love (page 83)

God, what can I do today for the man who is still sick? (page 164)

If you have resentment that you want to be free of, pray:

God, I ask that everything I want for myself be given _____, I ask for _____'s health, prosperity, and happiness (page 552)

Also select and memorize a few set prayers which emphasize the principles in the Big Book, such as the Step 3 Prayer (page 63), the Step 7 Prayer (page 76), the St. Francis Prayer (AA12&12, page 99), the Serenity Prayer, or any other prayer.

Daily Prayer & Meditations

Big Book, pages 87-8;

Constantly remind yourself:

I am no longer running the show.

Say to yourself many times each day:

Thy will be done.

When agitated or doubtful:

God, please give me the right thought or action

Page 85 (thoughts which must go with you constantly):

How can I best serve thee?
Thy will (not mine) be done.

Page 67 (if a person offends you):

This is a sick man. How can I be helpful to him? God save me from being angry. Thy will be done.

Conclusion to Steps Ten and Eleven:

You can see that the Big Book leaves us plenty of time for doing things. It's not as if we spend a lot of time just meditating and praying. The Big Book is all about action!

If we do what the Big Book suggests, our Step Tens are done when we begin not to feel so spiritually fit, and doing them the Big Book way is pretty fast.

The three kinds of prayer and meditation of Step Eleven are really pretty quick too. We can do the nighttime one in five minutes in bed, the awakening one in five minutes, and the day-time ones in seconds, really. Keeping recovered doesn't seem to take much time!

That's very true in one way, of course. The Big Book does not seem to want us to spend a lot of time on internal thinking.

No, our main job, as the Big Book makes very clear, is to help others, not to waste our time thinking about ourselves.

The Big Book warns us at the end of the chapter on page 88: "But this is not all. There is action and more action. 'Faith without works is dead.' The next chapter is entirely devoted to Step Twelve."

The gatehouse of the Sieberling estate in Akron, Ohio, where Bill Wilson met Dr. Bob Smith.

Step Twelve—Introduction:

Why we have to carry the message:

On page 59 the Big Book tells us: "Half measures availed us nothing." Eleven-twelfth measures avail us nothing either. We can do the steps from One through Eleven, but if we don't get active and carry the message, we will die. It's that simple.

Let me start with quoting Doctor Bob in "Doctor Bob's Nightmare", the first story after the text of the Big Book. Doctor Bob, as many of you know, was the co-founder of AA:

> I spend a great deal of time passing on what I learned to others who want and need it badly. I do it for four reasons:
>
> 1. Sense of duty.
> 2. It is a pleasure.
> 3. Because in so doing I am paying my debt to the man who took time to pass it on to me.
> 4. Because every time I do it I take out a little more insurance for myself against a possible slip.

The Big Book expresses this last thought very clearly. The beginning of Chapter 7, devoted entirely to Step Twelve, says at page 89: "Practical experience shows that nothing will so much insure immunity from drinking as intensive work with other alcoholics. It works when other activities fail."

If you look at the Step Three and the Step Seven prayers, you will see that they are really all about becoming fit to help other people. Look at the Step Three prayer at page 63: "Take away my difficulties, that victory over them may bear witness *to those I would help* of Thy Power, Thy Love, and Thy Way of life." We ask that our difficulties be taken away not for our own sake, but purely so that victory over our difficulties will show those whom we want to help the power of our higher power. And the Step Seven prayer at page 76: "I pray that you now remove from me every single defect of character which stands in the way of *my usefulness to you and my fellows*." We ask that those defects of character which hinder us from helping others be taken away from us.

Remember that at page 63 the Big Book tells us that when we follow the path of the steps, we have "a new Employer".

Chapter 7 is basically a manual on how to do our job. Our job description is actually found on page 102: "Your job now is to be at the place where you may be of maximum helpfulness to others."

We are disabled people. Other—"normal"—people don't have to do what we have to do. They don't have addiction problems. They can spend their spare time doing things they want to do for their own comfort and enjoyment.

But we cannot afford to do that. If we don't help others, we will relapse. We will go back to eating. And if we go back to eating, we will surely die. If you don't believe that by now, go back and think about Step One!

Dr. Bob says something else. He says it's a pleasure. He's right! We find that carrying the message gives us a sense of purpose, a sense of direction, and a sense of usefulness, all of which we need in our lives.

Some Step Twelve Promises:

Here are some promises of Step Twelve:

> Life will take on new meaning. To watch people recover, to see them help others, to watch loneliness vanish, to see a fellowship grow up about you, to have a host of friends—this is an experience you must not miss. (page 89)
>
> Follow the dictates of a Higher Power and you will presently live in a new and wonderful world, no matter what your present circumstances! (page 100)

So even though we HAVE to carry the message, it turns out that carrying the message becomes, for us, one of the most significant things that we do.

I know that is certainly true for me. I've done a lot of things in my life that other people would and have said should be fulfilling; but I never felt fulfilled doing them. I was always judging myself against impossible criteria and finding myself wanting.

But when I carry the message, I don't even have to be good at carrying the message to feel good about myself. I know I'm giving of myself without hope of reward or gain. It is the giving that is important, not how well the recipient is receiving the message.

And the most awful things that have happened to us or that we may have done to others now become a means of carrying the message of recovery to those who still suffer. One of the Promises is that "we will see how our experience can benefit others." And at page 124, the Big Book says:

> Showing others who suffer how we were given help is the very thing which makes life seem so worth while to us now. Cling to the thought that, in God's hands, *the dark past is the greatest possession you have*—the key to life and happiness for others. With it you can avert death and misery for them.

Meaning has now been given to our suffering or to the harms we've done others. We are different from what we used to be. The suffering we have undergone, or the harm we have done, were things that happened to someone we used to be, not to us.

We have the ability to say to those who still suffer that recovery is around the corner for them, that they can overcome whatever hands the past has dealt them!

We must not forget, however, the Big Book's statement on page 164: "you cannot transmit something you haven't got." It's important that we recover in order to be ABLE to carry the message!

With all that in mind, let's first of all look at the Big Book's instructions for carrying the message.

How to carry the message the Big Book way:

If you look at the early history of AA, you will see that carrying the message was almost a full-time occupation for AA pioneers. They would go to psychiatric wards or to hospitals for alcoholics and talk and talk and talk to the alcoholics who still suffered. And after those alcoholics were released, they would take those alcoholics home and talk and talk and talk.

Yet the Big Book's instructions are actually quite different. Here's the outline of the directions:

Pages 89 to 91: Finding the alcoholics to give the message to. Remember that the Big Book was written when AA was only in New York, Akron, and Cleveland. It was written as a textbook for those who did not have contact with AA and who did not have meetings to go to. So there necessarily had to be instructions for finding the right person. We're lucky in OA and in the other twelve-step programs—people come to us, and we don't have to find them. But if I moved to a place where there was no OA, I would follow the instructions on these pages. I won't discuss these pages any more, but for those of you who don't have OA in your area, these pages might come in very handy!

Pages 91 to 95: The first meeting. The actual instructions for explaining the program to the person who still suffers. I'll analyze this in some detail below.

Pages 96 to 98: guidelines for dealing with a sponsee. I'll spend a bit of time dealing with this.

Pages 98 to 100: general issues and the family of the person who is working the steps. I'll only deal with a few points here.

Pages 100 to 102: what recovery is like for us. I want to emphasize this area.

The first meeting (91 to 95):

The instructions are quite clear. (I'll translate them to compulsive eating.)

Tell your eating stories in such a way that the other person understands. Don't say anything about what you did to stop. Just tell your stories.

I will often start off by saying that I appreciate the opportunity to tell my story, because it helps me in my program. I then tell stories similar to the ones I told back in the first step—the hand going from food to mouth, from food to mouth, and not being able to stop it; my most disgusting eating stories; and my various attempts to lose weight, always undercut by my return to overeating.

Then describe yourself as a compulsive eater. Never comment on the other person. I will often say something like, "You're probably nothing like me, but I realized that I was a compulsive eater."

You talk about this from the basis of recovery. I talk about how freeing it has been to be able to have ice cream in the house and not to want to eat it, to watch other people eating foods that I used to binge on and be happy for them and not regret the fact that I can't eat that stuff.

Then talk about "how you finally learned that you were sick." (92) Talk about how you tried to stop but couldn't. I go into details on the many reasons I always slip. "I'm standing up so it doesn't count. I feel depressed. I've been good the last year or month or week or day or hour. I'll never have this taste again. It'll go to waste. Etc., etc."

Ultimately, talk explicitly about the allergy of the body and the obsession of the mind. I have worked on telling my story that way. I now tell my eating stories in such a way that they illustrate the two-fold nature of the problem. I first tell the stories of my uncontrollable binge eating and my complete inability to stop once I've started. Then I tell the stories of my yo-yo dieting and my complete inability to stop from starting again. These are the two problems—my physical cravings (allergy) and my mental obsession.

At this point the person will almost certainly be sharing his or her stories.

Then "begin to dwell on the hopeless feature of the malady." (92) This is extremely important. You tell your story in such a way that the other person understands that you—not him or her but you—were in the grips of a hopeless illness. So I will say something like, "I don't know about you, but I began to see how hopeless I was on my own, how I couldn't ever solve this problem on my own. I couldn't stop once I started to eat my binge foods, and I couldn't stop from starting again even if I'd managed to stop for a while. That explained my yo-yo dieting. It explained why I felt so defeated."

If the other person doesn't show interest, don't try to convince him or her. Just tell your story the best you can, thank the other person for letting you tell your story, say that if you can ever be of help, you're available, and then leave.

We don't try to recruit anyone. We don't tell everyone that OA is for them. It may not be. Nor should they come if they don't feel desperate. They'll come to meetings as hangers-on, but not as real members. They have to feel desperation, and it's our job to talk about that desperation.

So if the other person isn't interested, just leave.

But if the other person has ANY interest, that person will ask you how you recovered. *Then tell that person about the steps and how they worked for you.* The Big Book is clear that you don't hold anything back, that you don't sugar-coat the steps.

The Big Book talks about how to deal with the higher power issue with both agnostics and religious people on page 93. It's pretty blunt stuff.

For the agnostics you tell them that's no problem—it's their own conception of a higher power.

For the religious people you tell them that their religion certainly hasn't helped them at all, and they'd better remember that "faith without works is dead". And you go into detail about the inventory.

Here are some very important words on page 94:

> Outline the program of action, explaining how you made a self-appraisal, how you straightened out your past and why you are now endeavoring to be helpful to him. It is important for him to realize that your attempt to pass this on to him plays a vital part in your own recovery. Actually, he may be helping you more than you are helping him.

"He may be helping you more than you are helping him!" Of course that's true. I get something out of talking to the other person whether or not that person gets anything out of me. So I'm thankful for the opportunity to talk, to tell my story.

Then basically, after pleasantries, you leave! You don't continue the conversation, you don't try to be a friend, you've conveyed information about yourself and told the other person that if he or she is interested "you will do ANYTHING to help" (page 95).

If the other person is interested, you give him or her some homework—read the Big Book—and let that person initiate the next meeting. The Big Book cautions us against pushing the person at all, trying to rush that person into the program.

The Big Book thus describes a pretty short conversation—maybe a few hours at the most. Then it's up to the other person. Page 96:

> We find it a waste of time to keep chasing a man who cannot or will not work with you. If you leave such a person alone, he may soon become convinced that he cannot recover by himself. To spend too much time on any one situation is to deny some other alcoholic an opportunity to live and be happy.

This is pretty different from other methods of carrying the message I've experienced in OA, and actually quite different from what AAers did for the years prior to the publishing of the Big Book.

Basically, the initiative is up to the other person. You've made yourself available, and it's up to the other person to make use of your knowledge, IF he or she wants!

Other issues:

Once we begin to sponsor a willing sponsee, the Big Book makes it clear what our role is. We're there to share our experience on how to do the steps. That's it. A person who wants to follow the path we took is not following us, he or she is following the path we were taught by others.

The Big Book cautions us about having the other person become dependent on us. Page 98:

> The minute we put our work on a service plane, the alcoholic commences to rely upon our assistance rather than upon God. He clamors for this or that, claiming he cannot master alcohol until his material needs are cared for. Nonsense. [For Big Book trivialists, this is the shortest sentence in the Big Book!] Some of us have taken very hard knocks to learn this truth: Job or no job - wife or no wife - we simply do not stop drinking so long as we place dependence upon other people ahead of dependence on God. Burn the idea into the consciousness of every man that he can get well regardless of anyone. The only condition is that he trust in God and clean house.

This is an important message. It's not up to us to help the individual. We have to make certain that the people we sponsor do the steps. We have to make certain that they don't rely on us. I take that very seriously.

I sponsor by working through the Big Book. I don't do much phone-call sponsoring. I meet with my sponsees face to face. I don't REQUIRE them to do anything. They don't phone me every day, they don't check in with me. I'm there to help them work through the steps, and they can work through those steps however quickly or slowly they want to. (I caution them from my own experience how dangerous it is to work the steps slowly, because relapse is just around the corner.)

I work with them to develop a plan of eating that makes sense to them. I tell them that between the time they adopt a plan of eating (become abstinent) and the time they finish Step Nine, they are in a race to finish Step Nine before their mind persuades them to relapse. I tell them I'll do anything to help them keep abstinent. If that means they phone me every day, or phone me at 4:00 a.m. BEFORE they eat that doughnut, they can do that. And they can be assured of getting from me as much support as necessary. But whether they do phone me every day, or whether they phone me at 4:00 a.m. (no one ever has!) is up to them.

They do the work. I don't. I'm just there to share my experience. They sink or swim on their own, and I don't feel guilty if they sink. That's their problem and their responsibility, not mine. If they sink, maybe they'll get more desperate the next time and work harder.

That makes for pretty efficient sponsoring. Since I've been in recovery beginning sometime in May, 1993, I don't think I've ever turned down a sponsee. (I turned one down once before I really studied the Big Book, I think.) It has made for some work, but generally it works itself out, because I don't end up spending a great deal of time with my sponsees. I show them the way I was taught, and let them do the work.

When you come down to it, this method of sponsoring really means having the sponsee read the Big Book, and then meeting with the sponsee and leading the sponsee through what he or she has read, pointing out the directions contained in the book, and having the sponsee follow those directions.

Depending on the individual sponsee's ability to read and to retain what he or she has read, the actual total meeting time can vary between five and fifteen hours, spread over three to six meetings. The longest time is usually spent on Step Five, but even then the approach I've described doesn't usually take more than three, maybe four, hours.

I'm not suggesting that everyone should sponsor the way I do, but I am suggesting that, if you find yourself overloaded as a sponsor and unable to sponsor other people, you begin to analyze how you sponsor to see if there is a more efficient way.

The Promises of Recovery:

The Big Book's promise of recovery is quite clear and quite unconditional:

> Assuming we are spiritually fit, we can do all sorts of things alcoholics are not supposed to do. People have said we must not go where liquor is served; we must not have it in our homes; we must shun friends who drink; we must avoid moving pictures which show drinking scenes; we must not go into bars; our friends must hide their bottles if we go to their houses; we mustn't think or be reminded about alcohol at all. Our experience shows that this is not necessarily so. We meet these conditions every

> day. An alcoholic who cannot meet them, still has an alcoholic mind; there is something the matter with his spiritual status. (pages 100-101)

THIS is what the compulsive eater who still suffers wants to hear! There is no longer any fear. This is what distinguishes a Twelve-Step program from any other program that deals with addictions—the actual freedom to be around the addictive substance or behavior and not want to indulge in it!

And the Big Book gives us guidelines for going to places where there is eating. We ask ourselves if we have "any good social, business or personal reason for going to this place?" (page 101) If we do, then we attend to that reason. If we don't, then we're shaky and we'd better find another compulsive eater to talk to!

Questions:

Here are a few questions for those who are ready to carry the message:

- Imagine that after a meeting you're talking with a newcomer who has only a few minutes to spend with you. How would you carry the message to that person?
- You may be the only example of the program someone who still suffers ever meets. How do you impart your recovery?
- How do you sponsor? Are you overwhelmed and aren't available to those who still suffer? Are the people you sponsor more dependent upon you than upon the steps and their higher power?

8 PHYSICIANS DRUG NEWS

The Charles B. Towns Treatment for Drug Addicts Alcoholics and Neurasthenics

Administered at

The Charles B. Towns Hospital,
NEW YORK

successfully and completely removes the poison from the system and obliterates all craving for drugs and alcohol.

Because of its efficiency and thoroughness, its disclosure, freely and voluntarily, to the medical profession, and the consistent adherence by the principals to ethical standards in its application and advancement, the Charles B. Towns treatment, together with its parent institution, enjoys the confidence, cooperation and support of clinicians of national prominence.

And because it has withstood the searchlight of critical and discriminating investigation and the sure test of fourteen years' practical application, it commands your confidence.

There is nothing, therefore, about this treatment that is secret, it has been revealed thoroughly in articles which have appeared in the Journal A. M. A. and elsewhere.

The coupon below will make it convenient for you to ask for reprints of these articles and descriptive booklet.

The Charles B. Towns Hospital P.D.N.
293 Central Park West, NEW YORK
Please send me Reprints and Booklet,
M.D

Tradition Five tells us that the primary purpose of every OA meeting is to carry the message of recovery to those who still suffer.

A proper study of that tradition would put an end to a lot of debate that goes on in OA about "Tradition Violations".

The real issue in so many of those debates is whether or not something helps or hinders carrying the message.

We don't need "Traditions Police" in our program. We need people who work hard to figure out how to carry our message well. We can't carry it well if we go against the traditions that provide us with unity. But that doesn't mean that every time someone does something different it's automatically a "violation" of a tradition!

Step Twelve Continued:

As the Foreword to the First Edition says, "we have recovered from a seemingly hopeless state of mind and body." And the promises of this recovery are the freedom from the bondage of self and the freedom from the bondage of food.

As the Big Book reminds us, however, "it is easy to let up on the spiritual program of action and rest on our laurels." (page 85) Although we have recovered, "we are not cured of alcoholism. What we really have is a daily reprieve contingent on the maintenance of our spiritual condition." (page 85)

The first two bulwarks of this reprieve are continuing to clean house (Step Ten) and trusting in our higher power (Step Eleven). The last bulwark is our job in life—to "be of maximum helpfulness to others" (page 102). That's what Step Twelve is about.

In this chapter I might be kind of provocative. If I am, please just remember to take what you like (and maybe what you don't like!) and leave the rest. Take a Step Four through Nine and call me in the morning!

It's all fun from here on in! We've recovered, and we're happy, joyous, and free.

The responsibility for achieving a healthy body weight:

If we are to be of maximum helpfulness to others, we must carry the message to the compulsive eater who still suffers, and we must carry that message to the best of our abilities. What kind of a message are we carrying to the newcomer in our room, or to the person who has been coming for some time but hasn't yet worked the steps, if we are not working towards a healthy body weight?

The compulsive eater who still suffers wants one thing—normalcy. Now normalcy has two parts.

The first is the practical one—the certainty that working the steps will allow that person to look normal, to lose weight if he or she is overweight, and to gain weight if he or she is underweight.

The second is the one the compulsive eater who still suffers has never had from any other diet program—the spiritual sanity that provides freedom from food.

We have to model both of those if we are to be of maximum helpfulness to others. We should neither be living in fat serenity nor be white-knuckle abstaining

We don't have to be thin to sponsor. Not at all. A person who has 300 pounds to lose/release and who has recovered within months, and is losing weight, is a tremendous inspiration, even if still morbidly obese. And there are people whose medical condition is such that they can lose no more weight, but if they have recovered, they can sponsor beautifully.

What I am talking about, however—and I have myself been an example of this—are people who talk about how they have been members of this program for a long time, how they have recovered, how food is no longer an issue for them, but who do not appear to have a healthy weight.

The question they must ask themselves—as I asked myself—is how *well* they are carrying the message. Are they carrying the message to the best of their ability? I know when I was among them I was not carrying the message well.

On the other hand, having a healthy weight does not necessarily provide the message either.

We have to have recovered from the freedom of the bondage of food and of self. We can use OA as a diet support group without doing the steps. We can be the OA equivalent of dry drunks—white-knuckle abstainers. That isn't a very effective message either.

Recovery from compulsive eating is a product of the spiritual awakening we have received from the Twelve Steps. It is certainly *not* weight loss without the steps. And it's my experience that neither is it the steps without working toward a healthy body weight.

Now that the definition of "abstinence" has been changed by the group conscience of OA to "the action of refraining from compulsive eating and compulsive food behaviors while working towards or maintaining a healthy body weight", it's clear that if we claim to be abstinent we must also be working towards or maintaining a healthy body weight.

Service is different from twelfth step work:

Step Twelve tells us we have to carry the message. That is sponsoring. That is speaking at meetings about our recovery. That is speaking to newcomers or members who are still suffering after the meeting. That is phoning people and meeting people between meetings. That is speaking at workshops. That is leading workshops.

There is also the work of keeping OA alive. That is unlocking the door, setting up the chairs, making the coffee, publicizing meetings, getting involved in Intergroup, Region, or World Service.

Because the primary purpose of every meeting in OA and of OA itself is to carry the message, keeping OA alive through the meetings and the structure of OA is vitally important.

In and of itself doing this kind of work, however, is *not* carrying the message; it is merely helping to keep alive a structure in which the message CAN be carried. There's a big difference. Let me give you an example.

When I was relapsing, I was responsible for a meeting. I unlocked the door, put up the signs, arranged the chairs, kept the meeting record, paid the bills, etc. But I was in relapse. I was carrying the wrong message.

When it became clear that the meeting was in trouble (I was the only constant attendee) I began to look at the reason; and it wasn't far off—I simply had to look in the mirror!

Sure, I was frantically doing service to keep the meeting alive, but the meeting was of no value because its only constant attendee was not carrying the message of recovery. As a matter of fact, by talking the talk but not walking the walk, I was carrying a message of hopelessness.

More than that, doing all this work wasn't giving me any recovery whatsoever!

I was doing harm to OA, when you come down to it. I was talking about how wonderful OA was, when it was apparent to everyone except me that OA wasn't working for me. Really, I wasn't working the steps, so of course OA wasn't working for me.

So newcomers who came to the meeting were scared off. Not just from that meeting, but probably from OA as a whole. My service work was not getting me slim, and it was scaring away prospective members.

So there's a big difference between service and Twelfth Step work!

How do we carry the message in our meetings?:

On page 133, the Big Book tells us: "We are sure God wants us to be happy, joyous, and free." On page 160, the Big Book describes how a newcomer sees an AA meeting: "He succumbed to that gay crowd inside, who laughed at their own misfortunes and understood his."

- Are your meetings happy and joyous and free?
- Do they talk about recovery?
- Are they meetings where the very format itself discourages crosstalk and whining?
- At a break, or at the end of the meeting, are newcomers surrounded by people who want to help them, or are they ignored because longer-term members are talking to each other?
- Does the format stress doing the steps to reach recovery?
- Are there enough sponsors for the newcomers?
- Is there laughter?
- Is there a sense of recovery?
- Do people willingly pitch in?

Now that I've recovered, I go to meetings not to get something from them but to give away what was so freely given to me. I'm lucky to live in a city where there are OA meetings. I don't have to scour the food buffets or go to the eating disorder clinics to find someone to carry the message to. I just have to go to meetings to find someone to carry the message to.

So I suggest you think about your meetings and how well they carry the message.

What if you're in a meeting that doesn't in your opinion carry a message that grabs the newcomers? What are your options?

I would never consider the following options without putting that meeting, and perhaps some of its members, into a Step 10 Resentment and Fear consideration. Only that gives me the clarity of mind to consider these options.

You may find yourself guided to get *more* involved rather than less involved. Sure, a meeting which is sick might be on its deathbed and it might be reasonable simply not to support it and let it die. But — and especially if it's the only meeting available to you—maybe, just maybe, it needs a lot of love and honesty—it needs that unique quality that you, as a recovered compulsive eater, can give!

Consider as well that you may simply be wrong about that meeting. Maybe it's a perfectly good meeting and you just have some control issues! (I know this is a real possibility, because it has been true for me!) You should discuss your feelings with someone you know who has what you want to see if you're right or wrong about the quality of a meeting.

But if you're right, and it is not a good meeting, you have three major options.

1. You can simply not go to the meeting. I do not recommend this option if there are no other meetings available. I have been in correspondence with people who have said that they like online meetings because they don't like the meetings available in their area. They are missing marvellous opportunities to carry the message, I think. Moreover, you risk isolation by not dealing with your resentments.

2. You can try to change the format of the meeting by asking for a business meeting and asking the meeting to go through a group inventory about how well the group is going. Focusing on Tradition Five will assist in having people think about whether the group is doing well.

3. You can carry the message your own way no matter what else the meeting is about. You can make certain that your sharing focuses on recovery through the steps. You can reach out to newcomers. You can mention the Big Book. The group conscience of OA, the World Service Business Conference, has said clearly that no one should be restricted from speaking at any OA meeting because of a difference in approach to the program.

OA in general:

OA has been going through some transition phases. Back in the 1980s we had many more members than we have now. We started to decline in the early 1990s, but our membership appears to be increasing these days.

As I look back in my years in OA, I think I can see the roots of the decline in a few things:

- When the OA 12 & 12 came out, many people thought it replaced the Big Book. The Board of Trustees put out the Twelfth Step Workbook and the Step Four Inventory Guide, both of them NOT Conference-approved. Many people stopped using the directions in the Big Book.
- Our major growth didn't necessarily mean major recovery. It is entirely possible that many people came into OA and didn't do the steps and didn't recover, or relapsed. So when we "lost" members, in fact we were simply reverting back to a natural growth. To grow quickly we ultimately need a lot of recovered members who will help those who still suffer.
- Unlike AA and most other Twelve-Step groups, we have two major industries—the food industry and the diet industry—as well as professions—like dietitians and doctors—who try to persuade us that we can eat everything, even our binge foods, in moderation, that our only problem is control, so-called "won't power". This feeds into our mental obsession.
- We tend to be nice in OA. We tend to be welcoming and supportive, which is good, but we aren't always direct. We have (I have) a tendency to be wishy-washy and vague so no one is offended. Sometimes our literature reflects that.

I think our increase in members now is attributable to a growing emphasis on the Big Book's set of directions, much clearer literature that talks of recovery and the double whammy of the physical cravings and mental obsession, and a growing sense of hopelessness among newcomers that other methods they've tried simply aren't working.

OA belongs to us, the members. We have to make certain that it reflects our best practices, that we don't let it stray from its one message—that the Steps work! That's why we have to get involved at all levels, including World Service, to make certain that OA reflects our message of recovery.

The Twelve Provocations:

Here are twelve provocative propositions, with my annotations to show how I've arrived at each of the propositions:

1. I am a RECOVERED compulsive eater, not a recovering one.

ANNOTATION: In relation to a person who has worked the Twelve Steps and is free from the bondage of addiction, the Big Book consistently uses the word "recovered" and not "recovering". The word "recovering" is used only once, and then only to describe someone who is still working through the Steps and is not yet free from the bondage of addiction. The Big Book uses "recovered" because that word shows a complete change in one's attitude. It is *the* advertisement to the compulsive overeater who still suffers. I no longer have the illness I used to have. True, it's a bite away. True, it's a "daily reprieve contingent" on my spirituality. But right now, for the *moment*, I have recovered from a seemingly hopeless condition of mind and body. The compulsive eater who still suffers deserves no less from me. I am not full of pride. I am humbled by the clear knowledge that I was unable to accomplish this on my own; I had to surrender completely and admit that I was powerless; and only then could I begin to find the power that has caused my recovery.

2. Abstinence is NOT the most important thing in my life without exception; the consciousness of the presence of God is.

ANNOTATION: Page 51: "When many hundreds of people are able to say that the consciousness of the Presence of God is today the most important fact of their lives . . . " The point is that so long as I live on a spiritual basis working the Twelve Steps, I am sane in relation to food. So long as I am sane, I am free from any temptation to return to the insanity of the food. Therefore I am abstinent. It's not because I work at being abstinent. It's because I work at being *sane*!

3. Although a sponsor, if available, is very important for recovery, a sponsor is not NECESSARY to recover.

ANNOTATION: The Big Book was written as a textbook for people who had no sponsors. Its instructions work even if there are no sponsors available. The point of this proposition is that no one should use the lack of sponsors as an EXCUSE not to do the steps. No one should be dependent on another person for recovery. If I depend on a sponsor, then where is my dependence on a higher power? Page 98: "we simply do not stop drinking so long as we place dependence upon other people ahead of dependence on God. Burn the idea into the consciousness of every man that he can get well regardless of anyone. The only condition is that he trust in God and clean house."

4. You can recover in WEEKS.

ANNOTATION: It is possible for most people, using the instructions in the Big Book, to finish off Step Nine within two months. If working the steps is a priority for you—and it certainly should be if you are a member of OA!—you can make the time that's necessary. What, after all, takes time? Step Three is a prayer said in a minute. Writing Step Four can take a week or so, but there's not a lot of writing using the forms provided. Step Five using those forms (and not reading Columns Two and Three of the Resentment Form) shouldn't take more than four or five hours. Steps Six, Seven, and Eight, are done the same day as Step Five. Step Nine may take a while simply because of the availability of people, but the bulk can be done relatively quickly. Then you should have recovered. Steps Ten, Eleven, and Twelve, keep you recovered.

5. The Tools of Recovery are NOT an essential part of the OA program.

ANNOTATION: All OA stands for is the Twelve Steps of Recovery. The Tools pamphlet is helpful if a person has adopted a plan of eating and has not yet recovered—in that case the Tools provide things for people to do instead of eating compulsively. But the Tools are not a substitute for the steps. It is true that working the steps may often involve using a tool. Doing Step Four and Step Ten means that you'll be Writing. Sponsoring means you'll be using the Telephone and going to Meetings and Sponsoring. Working the Steps means you'll be reading Literature. But the point is that you're doing the STEPS, not doing a tool.

6. You DON'T take Steps One and Two.

ANNOTATION: Steps One and Two are *acknowledgement* steps. You study them to understand the Problem (Step One), which is Powerlessness, and the Solution (Step Two), which is Power. But the Big Book has no instructions for doing Steps One or Two. As a matter of fact, Step Two is not even mentioned as a step in the text of the Big Book other than in the list of steps on page 59.

7. Steps Three, Six, Seven, and Eight, should *not* take a long time to get through.

ANNOTATION: These are the steps which Bill put in to make certain there were no loopholes. The instructions for them in the Big Book certainly indicate that they are not the *huge* steps that some commentaries have made. They are stations on the way; you have to pay attention to them and be conscious of them; but they should not take a long time if you work the steps the Big Book way.

8. You *don't* make amends to yourself.

ANNOTATION: We often hear, "the first person I have to make amends to is myself", and what that is code for is "I have to learn to say no, I have to learn to take care of myself." The Big Book is outer-directed, not inward-directed. Sure, you have to take care of yourself—but that's because you have an obligation to carry the message, and how can you carry the message well if you're not in good shape. And you *should* be saying no if saying yes would allow another person to come to harm, as it often does when people exploit your people-pleasing nature and they harm themselves by doing harm to you. But notice how this is all recast into thinking about others and not yourself. If there is anything the Big Book stands for, it is that your needs and your ego should not stand in the way of being useful to your higher power. Now, it is absolutely true that you end up making amends to yourself by making amends to those you have harmed. Because amends to those you have harmed allows your character defects to be removed. And having your character defects removed is in fact the greatest amends you can make to yourself!

9. You should NOT sponsor until after you have completed Step Nine.

In this context "sponsor" means carrying the message. ANNOTATION: Page 164: "Obviously you cannot transmit something you haven't got." If you have not recovered, you can still be helpful to people (there are meetings where no one has recovered, and at those meetings people help each other out), but the Big Book is clear that what appeals to the compulsive eater who still suffers is a person who has been there, but isn't "there" any more, someone who has recovered from a seemingly hopeless condition of mind and body.

10. Service is NOT slimming.

ANNOTATION: "Service", as I've discussed above, is to be distinguished from "carrying the message" through sponsorship and outreach. Carrying the message is one of the prerequisites for continuing recovery. As Dr. Bob is reputed to have said: Clean House (Step Ten), Trust God (Step Eleven), Help Others (Step Twelve). Helping OA out is a way of making certain that OA carries the message as well. But there are "service junkies" in OA who think that doing service will give them recovery. It doesn't, at least from the Big Book perspective. It provides the method for carrying the message, and carrying the message *keeps* our recovery because it's Step Twelve, but Steps Four through Nine are what *bring* us recovery. And doing just Steps One and Twelve will not bring about recovery.

11. Food CAN be discussed at meetings.

ANNOTATION: Page 101: "In our belief any scheme of combating alcoholism which proposes to shield the sick man from temptation is doomed to failure." How do you think it would sound if at an AA meeting someone said, "And then I picked up a glass filled with a yellow fizzy liquid and drank it?" If people who have not recovered get uneasy with stories about food, then that's their problem. And if they eat over it, then maybe they'll get desperate enough to do the steps, which will bring them recovery.

12. Every person who wants to be a member of OA should know exactly what having "a desire to stop eating compulsively" means.

ANNOTATION: Page 96: "We find it a waste of time to keep chasing a man who cannot or will not work with you. If you leave such a person alone, he may soon become convinced that he cannot recover by himself. To spend too much time on any one situation is to deny some other alcoholic an opportunity to live and be happy."

I come at this from a personal perspective. I was in relapse and was dying in this program. But if people asked me how I was, I would tell them, "Fine!" and they would say, "Great to hear that. Keep coming back! We love you. Love to hear you talk." One day the shyest person in the room asked me how I was, but this time when I said, "Fine!", she said, "I mean REALLY!" And I fell apart and admitted I was in trouble. She was courageous and loving enough to confront me, and if she hadn't, I have no idea whether I would ever have emerged from relapse.

Certainly I would have been in relapse much much longer and might have done permanent damage to my body. But if I hadn't broken down and admitted I was in trouble, and if instead I had said to her, "You have no right to take my inventory!" then I would have gone back to eating badly; perhaps I would then have finally realized that I was powerless over food, that my life was unmanageable.

The Big Book is clear that we have a duty to be honest and straightforward. And if people are using our meetings as coffee klatsches or pity pots and aren't doing the steps, why aren't we confronting them with love and compassion, why aren't we making it uncomfortable for them just to wallow in self-pity and fat?

There are a lot of groups that offer support for weight loss. We offer something else in addition to that support – the Twelve Steps that give us freedom from compulsive eating. That's different from support. Some people need only some support, only some guidance about what to eat and how much to eat, only some sense of encouragement. That's not what OA is about. It's about the Twelve Steps and it's for people who are addicted.

Sure, Tradition Three tells us that the only requirement for OA membership is the desire to stop eating compulsively. But doesn't each person who attends our meetings owe it to us and to OA as a whole to consider whether he or she REALLY wants to stop eating compulsively? And doesn't each meeting owe to any prospective compulsive eater an explanation of exactly what it means to have a desire to stop eating compulsively?

It isn't enough to want to diet, to lose weight, to be lonely and want a support group. To stop eating compulsively means to be free from the obsession that keeps returning us to eating foods, food ingredients, and/or eating behaviors that cause us uncontrollable cravings. We owe a responsibility to make that clear.

Conclusion:

The Big Book is tough. It's down to earth. It doesn't mince words. I once heard something like this in OA: "Truth without compassion is cruel. Compassion without truth is harmful." Certainly everything we say has to be full of love and tolerance and compassion. But we harm people if we don't tell them the truth. And as people-pleasers, many of us in OA may know how to do the compassion bit, but we shy away from the truth bit.

So let's think about how we treat our fellow-OAer who's still suffering. Are we killing that person with kindness?

Questions:

Here are some questions:

- What do you think about the proposition that a recovered OA member owes a duty to reach a healthy body weight?

The headstones of Dr. Bob and Bill W. Neither mentions the pivotal role they played as co-founders of AA.

- What are the strong points of the meetings you go to? What are the weak points?
- Do the meetings you go to make doing the steps a priority? If not, what do they do, and what do you think about that?
- Are you a service junkie? Why?
- Do you know people in OA who are being killed with kindness, who are clearly relapsing or not doing the steps, and who are not being confronted with love? What ideas do you have for talking to people like that?

Questions and responses:

Here are some questions I was asked toward the end of the Step Study I did online, on which this booklet has been based, and my responses to each of them:

How do we get abstinent before doing the steps?:

I'm having a hard time with the concept of abstinence. For me, that means refraining from eating my 'trigger foods', the ones that cause me to relapse. I understand abstinence is essential for AA, NA, etc. They have to stop drinking, stop using, and I have to stop eating my trigger foods. I understand that this needs to be done BEFORE we can be actively 'working the Steps'. My question is how do we do that, without working the Steps? Isn't that the same as willpower? And the BB tells us that willpower never works for us. (IT sure doesn't for me, either!) To "just say no" seems so much like willpower, and combined with a food plan, sounds just like all the diets I've ever tried. So how do we get abstinence? And does abstinence mean the end of cravings? Mine haven't ended. They are less frequent now, and a little easier to resist, at times. But I still have them and still give in to them, so I relapse often and have to start the Steps over again. So what is the answer about abstinence?

RESPONSE: I appreciate this question because it allows me to clarify my thinking. How do we get abstinent before doing the Steps? We become desperate enough about our own inability to control our food, and hopeful that if we can keep to our plan of eating for a few weeks or a few months and work the Steps to the best of our ability, we will finally be free of the food.

It's NOT willpower. It's desperation. It's hanging in there. It's just a day at a time. This is not the condition we're striving toward. It's just a temporary thing.

We do whatever we have to do to keep abstinent while we're working the Steps. If that means we have a food buddy, or that we weigh and measure, or that we rid our home of our binge foods, or whatever—we do what we have to do. Cravings are cravings. They don't have to be fulfilled. To give in to our cravings is, of course, the essence of our mental obsession.

So I don't have an easy answer. The person who wrote has to be so desperate that he or she will do ANYTHING to stop eating compulsively AND to work the steps. One thing I can suggest is to work out a plan. First, what is my plan for doing the steps? Do I have a sponsor, can I make an appointment for doing Steps Three and Step Five with that person, so that I have something to look forward to? Second, what is my plan for not eating compulsively? What tools should I use? What help can I get? It's just a matter of weeks before I'll recover. What can I do for that short time while I'm working on my steps?

Abstinence may or may not mean the end of cravings. It means only the end of compulsive eating. Our bodies may still be quite hooked, or they may after a time not react quite the same. They're two different things.

It may be that the writer is using the word "cravings" to describe the mental obsession that keeps us going back to food. That is guaranteed to go away, a day at a time, when we have finished Step Nine. The key is getting to Step Nine as soon as possible.

How can a person with deep spiritual beliefs not believe in God?:

You wrote in Step 1: "I'm Jewish (but an agnostic, which I'll talk about when we get to Step Two)" And in Step 12: "2. Abstinence is NOT the most important thing in my life without exception; the consciousness of the presence of God is." If you are Agnostic, which means that you suspend judgment, saying that there are not sufficient grounds either for affirmation or for denial of God, it seems you are not Agnostic at all. If the consciousness of the presence of God is the most important thing in your life, this just doesn't sound like words of an Agnostic, but those of someone who has a deep faith that there is a God. So my question is, would you make me understand how you resolve those two seemingly conflicting statements? I have a deep personal interest in this because, while I was raised Presbyterian, minored in religion in college and converted to Catholicism as a young adult, I consider myself an Agnostic, not religious at all but with a deep spiritual side.

RESPONSE: I am indeed an agnostic. There are no sufficient grounds, in my opinion for affirmation or denial of God.

Outside of twelve-step fellowships, the word "God" means "a personal omnipotent person or persons or thing". When I speak to someone who's not a member of OA or any other Twelve Step Fellowship, I say clearly that I am an agnostic.

In OA, however, "God" doesn't mean what it means in the outside world. "God" means "anything of my own understanding which is higher (or more important) than I am".

That was the question my first sponsor asked me: Is there anything that is more important than I am? Well, sure there is! I have all kinds of beliefs in things that, if put to the test, I'd like to think I would consider more important than even my life. Certainly I am morally certain that I would give up my life for my wife or my daughters. So clearly love is more important than I am. And theoretically (because I've never had to face the issue) I'd like to think that I am courageous enough to die for truth or justice. And beautiful things overwhelm me and make me feel very humble, so that I believe that beauty is something that is more important than I am.

So I have decided that my Higher Power consists of the abstract notions of Truth, Love, Justice, and Beauty. From "We Agnostics" in the Big Book I take it that my problem is that I have blocked myself off from Truth, Love, Justice, and Beauty—or what I will call God according to the Third and Eleventh Step. As I work the steps, and my defects of character are removed by Step Nine, I am no longer blocked, and Truth, Love, Justice, and Beauty become my guides in life. I live my life for those concepts and not for myself or for my own ideas of what should be.

When people who believe in a personal God say they get their "direction" from God, their concept seems to me that they feel as if they are "pushed" into a certain direction. I get my direction from Truth, Love, Justice, and Beauty, by using those concepts as a kind of a magnetic North Pole—they are the direction I go toward.

Sure, I have to make adjustments in reading the Big Book, which was, truth to tell, written by middle-aged ex-gutter-drunk white Christians who tried their best to be as inclusive as possible, but didn't always succeed. But I'm not perfect either, and I understand, from their attempts to be inclusive, that they had the best of intentions!

Amends to yourself?:

You said "8. You DON'T make amends to yourself." Tell me why my thinking on this is wrong because I go by that phrase in the prayer "The Our Father"—"Forgive us our trespasses AS WE FORGIVE THOSE who have trespassed upon us". Wouldn't then forgiving others first, then be making amends to myself? I thought that by stopping/or changing my self-abusive behavior, I was making amends to myself?

RESPONSE: Yes, precisely! By changing our behavior we make amends to ourselves. But we change our behavior in order to undo the harms we have caused others! We look outward not inward! We don't try to make amends to ourselves. We make amends to others, and in doing so, change ourselves into different people—people who are not blocked off from the sunlight of the spirit by selfishness, dishonesty, self-seeking, and fear.

My proposition that "you don't make amends to yourself" is intended to deal with the quite popular concept that we have to take actions that make us FEEL better. The only way that we will ultimately feel better is to make amends to others, and thus have our character defects removed. It is true that in making amends to others, I may take actions that ultimately benefit me; I may say no to people whom I used to enable; I may take personal time to get into better shape and to relax. But the REASON I am doing those things is to help others and to make amends. My job is to be of maximum helpfulness to others, the Big Book says at page 102. That is what I have to keep in mind!

Difference between Step 10 and before nighttime Step 11 inventories:

My question is: Am I doing a Step 10, including Steps 4-9, when I do a Step 11, including Steps 4-9, the way the Step Eleven form suggests for Evening Meditation? When I take a Step 10 am I automatically doing a Step 11? I know that there are two different sets of questions for each Step. Does 10 supersede 11 or vice versa?

RESPONSE: There is one major similarity between Step Ten /and the nighttime Step Eleven, but many major differences. At least that's how I see it, and I could be wrong!

Similarity: they both incorporate the concepts of doing Steps Four through Nine.

Differences: The Step Eleven meditation is not done on paper, deals only with the past day, is done daily, and doesn't necessarily require a Step Five. Step Ten is done on paper (using the forms or at least the BB instructions), is done as needed, requires a formal Step Five, and deals with anything that is on your mind.

Practically speaking, Step Ten is a "mop-up"—that is, it picks up on the long-term issues that weren't covered in Step Eleven. Practically speaking, the more carefully you do Step Eleven, the fewer Step Tens you will probably have to do!

Here's an example. My mother was quite ill for four years, and in those four years my father spent a great deal of energy taking care of her. Every day I might do a Step Eleven thinking about her and my father, but it would be in the context of THAT day. I would think of any interactions I had with either of them, or whether I had even spoken to or seen them that day.

But every so often, when I found myself getting very moody, I would do a Step Ten and just put my mother and my father down on the resentment form. I would discover a whole bunch of long-range issues dealing with my entire reaction to my mother's illness and my father's role as well—things relating to self-pity (I don't have the mother of my childhood) to fear (will it hurt my father's relationship with my mother) to selfishness (I just don't want her sick). So the Step Ten was a big one. My Step Elevens dealt with day-to-day issues.

That, at any rate, is how I see it. But many Big Book thumpers actually see the nighttime Step Eleven as being an occasion for doing a complete Step Ten, writing things down on paper and phoning their sponsors and working out Steps Eight & Nine, every day.

If you're not a normal weight are you credible?:

I was feeling a bit let down by your last post. It seems to me that you are saying if a person is not a normal weight, whatever that means, is not very credible to others at meetings. I have been in program since 1991 and have had success in losing weight. I did however use OA as a diet. It wasn't until three years ago that I immersed myself in the BB step study process. I studied and worked very hard at it. I was sick last winter and was housebound for over three months. I could not go to meetings all winter long and as a result, I went into relapse. I am fighting my way out of it now. You alluded to being in relapse so you must understand what that feels like. I hate going to my old meetings because of my weight. Right now I need encouragement from people like yourself who have walked my path. I do have spiritual recovery and people do have respect for me. I feel like I've been put under a microscope after I read your post. I hope and pray that I will regain the willingness I had years ago and will go forward.

RESPONSE: I am very sorry that I didn't make myself clear in a number of ways. I think it is wonderful that this person is fighting his/her way out of relapse; I have indeed been in relapse and know how difficult it is.

I want to make it clear that the first issue is not how much weight one has lost (assuming one was overweight), but whether that person has recovered through the Twelve Steps.

If a person has recovered through the Twelve Steps—and remember, when I use the word "recovered", I mean that the person has had "the personality change sufficient to bring about recovery from" compulsive eating (the definition from the Appendix on Spiritual Experience)—then that person is able to help others and be an inspiration to others. I trust that is what this person means by having achieved "spiritual recovery".

The second issue comes AFTER recovery. That comes from my suggestion that we have a duty to be a model in the program in order to help the newcomer. And that means, I think, that we have a duty to WORK TOWARDS a healthy body weight. It doesn't mean we have to BE at a healthy body weight in order to help the newcomer. It means we have to work TOWARDS a healthy body weight. Note I say "healthy" and not "normal" or "thin".

I have met many people in the program who have been morbidly obese who have recovered. They have lost 100 or 200 or 300 pounds but they are still working towards losing hundreds more. Even obese, they are inspirations. They are beacons of hope to so many people who are morbidly obese.

And I know others who are tremendously overweight but have worked the steps quickly and have achieved recovery; but they are also working towards losing much more weight. And they are inspirations as well.

As well, I know people who have recovered who simply can't achieve a healthy body weight, for various medical reasons. They might be taking medication. Their metabolism might be shut down. There may be many other reasons. And they're inspirations as well.

In meetings and one-on-one all of these people explain, however, that they have recovered from the bondage of food but are still in the process of losing their weight or just physically cannot lose any more weight.

They do that because they feel an OBLIGATION to provide hope to the newcomer who still suffers. And what kind of hope is there if a person who is grossly overweight talks to a newcomer who wants to lose weight about how wonderful the Twelve Steps are, if that person doesn't explain his or her condition?

Step Twelve tells me to carry the message of recovery to those who still suffer. I believe that means I have to carry it to the best of my ability. To carry it to the best of my ability means that I cannot be content to have achieved freedom from the bondage of food without working to make certain that it shows on me physically.

I hope that's clearer. I don't think anyone need feel defensive in this program. We are all who we are, all joining together because we have a desire to stop eating compulsively. We have an obligation to be loving and honest, but we don't have a right to judge anyone else. But I have no problem with suggesting that each recovered OAer reflect on whether he or she is doing everything possible to carry the best message.

Ultimately the people we have to think about most are compulsive eaters who still suffer. They are the most important people in the room. We have to make certain that they see hope in the rooms!

The definition of "abstinence" has been changed by the group conscience of OA to be: "Abstinence in Overeaters Anonymous is the action of refraining from compulsive eating and compulsive food behaviors while working towards or maintaining a healthy body weight." This emphasizes the importance our group conscience gives to reaching and maintaining a healthy body weight. It is our responsibility to do so!

The issue of service:

You wrote: "I was doing harm to OA, when you come down to it. I was talking about how wonderful OA was, when it was apparent to everyone except me that OA wasn't working for me. Really, I wasn't working the steps, so of course OA wasn't working for me. So newcomers who came to the meeting were scared off. Not just from that meeting, but probably from OA as a whole. My service work was not getting me slim, and it was scaring away prospective members." We have many Trusted Servants and need many more. They are receiving a mixed message. For example, a secretary of a support group begins to slip and heads into relapse. We get a letter—"Sorry, I must leave. I owe it to my recovery." So, the busiest among us begin looking for replacements or doing it ourselves. They announce their departure and why to their Trusted Servant list and, like dominoes, others follow suit. Multiply this many times over,and pretty soon we find ourselves with our main job being finding people to welcome newcomers, say goodbye to others, lead meetings and dozens of other things. And the end result is that the division of labor becomes so much for some that burn-out occurs as they try to keep their support group going so that those who need to leave for their "recovery." So my question becomes: Do you feel someone who loves program, hates the non-abstinent state they're in, should leave their service job as a result?

RESPONSE: This is a good point. I'm sorry I didn't make myself clear. You don't have to be recovered to do a lot of service work in this program. It doesn't take recovery to be able to be responsible for the keys, making the coffee, putting out the literature, passing on announcements, collecting money, helping out at the silent auction or at the convention—in short, doing all the things that just keep OA running. And doing that kind of work can keep us busy and feeling responsible and feeling connected.

The Big Book says that we can't give away what we don't have; and that means that if we have not recovered, we can't carry the message of the Twelve Steps. But that doesn't mean we shouldn't help keep our lifeline, OA, alive!

When I said that "service isn't slimming" I meant only that service is not a SUBSTITUTE for doing the steps. Service can be an adjunct for doing the steps. It can help keep us from returning to the food WHILE we're doing the steps and recovering.

I also think this: if a meeting doesn't have enough people to perform all the functions of that meeting, then that meeting should consider whether it really needs all those functions or whether it should simply work on the recovery of its members. That's tough talk.

But if there aren't enough people to keep things going, then they should suffer the consequences of not having things kept going. Other people should not compensate for the lack of volunteers. If I have taken on a job, I'll do that job. But I'm not going to do three other jobs simply because the jobs exist!

In the end, an OA meeting needs very little to function other than a place and some publicity. Sure, it would be great to have regular business meetings. And sure, it is very important that literature be available and coffee be made. And it would be great to send someone to intergroup. But if not, then not!

And if intergroup doesn't have someone to buy literature or to put out the newsletter or to chair the meetings, then maybe intergroup should figure out why it needs to exist for the time being.

I believe that OA has to focus on recovery first. Everything else follows. I think that's why our membership is increasing after a large decline. We lost members over a decade ago. That meant that we couldn't do all the fantastic things that we had done before. We had to focus on keeping our shrinking meetings alive. And the only way to keep them alive was to work the Steps resolutely.

When we did that we recovered. And when we recovered we attracted more people. And when we attracted more people, our meetings grew stronger and there were more of them. And more people were available to do the jobs that were now needed.

They were doing them not to "do service" but because they recognized that OA was carrying a great message and was a beacon of hope for the compulsive eater who still suffers. Thus OA as a whole is beginning to prosper as a result.

The Twelve Steps do not belong to OA. We are simply guardians of the Twelve Steps. They have been entrusted to us. If we stray from them, we don't deserve to keep them as ours. If a meeting, or an intergroup, or even OA as a whole, isn't carrying a message of recovery, then its reason for existence is no longer valid. Luckily we are finding that we are carrying a great message of recovery, and therefore putting our energies into OA is worth while!

Constantly judged in meetings because of weight:

I feel I am constantly being judged by how much weight I am losing in the rooms, and they won't let you speak at some meetings until you get 30 days of abstinence. That, coupled with not being able to mention "food", who wants to talk anyway . . . at least in an AA meeting people can be honest, and share their "pain" openly, and not be reprimanded for it. The food obsession and sugar addiction has been harder for me than the alcohol, and I really don't feel supported in the rooms of OA. These internet meetings and step studies have helped me more than face to face meetings.

RESPONSE: As I explained in the last chapter the Big Book's approach to the steps certainly suggests that meetings should be able to mention specific foods. Fear is not a good reason for doing anything, and meetings that prohibit the mention of specific foods do not seem to me to be trusting that the message of recovery through the Twelve Steps will overcome fears like that.

It is against OA World Service Business Policy, the group conscience of OA, to prevent anyone from sharing at a meeting because of where they are in the program. I am sorry that there are meetings where people are actually prevented from speaking. I don't think that's particularly welcoming.

On the other hand, a meeting I go to recently voted to switch from going around the room to asking for volunteers to speak. That has had a fascinating effect on the meeting. The people who speak most often are those who are filled with enthusiasm and hope. Those who are feeling down find people to speak to after the meeting. Their hope doesn't come from speaking at a meeting or even sharing their feelings at a meeting. Their hope comes from the Twelve Steps.

Although OA meetings provide a great deal of support, they are not support groups. They are groups that are dedicated to carrying the message of recovery through the Twelve Steps of Overeaters Anonymous!

I want to talk more, though, about face to face meetings.

The importance of face to face meetings:

People have written in who say that they don't go to face to face meetings because the meetings aren't very good. I've also heard from people who say that there are no face to face meetings where they live. I want to talk about the importance of face to face meetings.

If I lived in a part of the world where there were no meetings at all, I would try to create them. I have to find compulsive eaters who still suffer. I have to carry the message of recovery to them. If there are no meetings where you live, you have a rare opportunity. You can be a founder! You can plant the seed in your own home ground!

It's not hard to start a meeting. It just requires some dedication. And that dedication comes from necessity. You'll die if you don't find some other compulsive eaters who still suffer!

What if you live in a place where there are meetings that appear to be crummy? Try to change them. I discussed this aspect last week in some detail. After you have analyzed your own motives and perspective through a Step Ten (Four through Nine) and have determined that the meetings really are not good, then start thinking about all those compulsive eaters who go to those meetings and never recover, or are completely turned off by what they think is OA and never return. Aren't you doing them harm by not helping them out? You could make certain that when you speak at one of those lousy meetings that you give a clear positive message. You could try to change the meeting through a group inventory. You could try to create a new meeting that gives a good message. You could volunteer to speak to the newcomer. You could make yourself available to sponsor. There are all kinds of ways for you to help the newcomer or the person who still suffers!

But you've having trouble recovering yourself because the meetings available to you don't have recovered people in them, and they're clique-ish, and they don't allow this or that to happen, and you can't share, and there's no one to sponsor, or no one recovered enough to sponsor, etc., etc. Well, the Big Book says you don't need a sponsor if you can't get one. There's no one else to blame but yourself. Do what the Big Book says. Recover. Then go to those meetings and make them better by your recovered presence!

But isn't it enough simply to type on my computer, to participate in these online meetings? I can't speak for everyone, of course. I know that for me, typing on the computer sometimes requires a great deal of concentration for me; but it also allows me to be distracted. With today's multi-tasking computers, I can be on a chatline, look at my e-mail, play solitaire, and have music playing. At a face to face OA meeting there are simply people who are recovering and people who are suffering, and they gather for only one purpose and do nothing else but try to fulfill that purpose.

More than that, when I'm on a computer I am physically isolated. For me, it's not much different from being on the phone. Both of those separate me from my body and from other people's bodies. I can't look people in the eye or hear their voices, or hug them, or hold their hands. I am limited in my sense and cannot be as sensitive to them as I would like to be.

I don't mean to denigrate online meetings. They provide all kinds of wonderful qualities. They are there when you need them. They provide a world of recovery that we often can't find in our little neck of the woods. They allow us to think a lot about what has been said because we can reread or listen to a recording of what has been said. And of course there are people who for many different reasons are simply physically unable to go to meetings. They may have a debilitating illness that immobilizes them. Online meetings are a godsend for them and a wonderful thing in and of themselves.

But if you are capable of going to a meeting, think about why you're not going to that meeting. Do a Step Four through Nine or a Step Ten on that issue. Are any of the reasons related to fear, or a sense of not being in control, or shame or guilt? Those are pretty heavy things to carry about!

Now that I have recovered on a daily basis, I do Steps Ten through Twelve to maintain my spiritual fitness. I clean house (Step Ten), I trust God (Step Eleven), and I help others (Step Twelve). I MUST do Step Twelve or I will lose my recovery! I don't want to do that.

Going to meetings is the easiest way to find people to help. I have to keep myself available. And the best way of doing that is by going to as many meetings as I can (without neglecting the obligations I owe to my work and my family and my friends) and carrying the best message I can.

How to talk to someone who's still suffering:

I've been asked by a number of people how to talk to someone who's been in the program for a long time and appears to be suffering, perhaps gaining weight, yet talks with a lot of authority about the program and the steps. Some OAers call these "fat serenity" people; the implication is that they talk a lot about serenity, and have simply learned to accept their overeating. Since I was certainly one of those people, I do have a process that you might consider.

The first suggestion is that you do or say nothing until you have done a Step Ten with that person or those people down as a resentment. Remember that Step Ten is Steps Four through Nine in the context of recovery. You MUST make certain that you have analyzed your own motives before you even do or say anything, and the only way I know how to do that is to go through Step Ten. Step Ten is the perfect way of making certain that anything you do you do for the good of other people, and not for your own comfort or sense of control.

If after going through Step Ten you come to the conclusion that you ultimately do more harm to those persons or to OA by remaining silent, than you would do harm by saying something and thus maybe hurting their feelings, then pray for the right thing to say.

Certainly one way of talking to people in that situation is: "I may be wrong, but I feel that you are having difficulties, and I would like to help you in whatever way I can." What if they are simply in denial and say, "No, I'm fine, no problems whatsoever"? You might be more direct and say, "You are visibly gaining weight; I'm concerned about your health. What is going on with you?"

Of course not everyone will suddenly respond as I did when confronted. Some people might simply say, "Thanks for being concerned, but I don't need any help." And maybe you're wrong and they don't need help. Or maybe you've just planted the seeds of doubt in them and they'll come to you or someone else for help in the future. Some people might be so offended that they don't come to meetings for a while; but they'll be back, this time realizing how resentments are killing them. At least you'll have done what you think is right!

Conclusion:

This is the end of the Step Study from a Big Book perspective. I want to emphasize that I am only a student and not a teacher. I am simply a recovered fat glutton who has been given a second chance in life and is trying to carry a message I have learned from others. I hope no one will be offended by anything I've said; but I hope people will be challenged by what I've said to figure out how—for them on a personal level—they can carry the message of recovery through the Twelve Steps to the best of their ability.

If you ever have any questions, please don't hesitate to contact me personally by e-mail at the link found at www.oabigbook.info. I love to hear about the spread of the Big Book's message of recovery within OA.

There are many ways of doing the Twelve Steps. I know people far more spiritual than I who didn't use the Big Book's set of instructions for doing the steps; so I know that the Big Book approach is only one of many. It has, however, two advantages. The first is that its approach to the problem and the solution—the simple concepts of the physical cravings and the mental obsession, and the spiritual solution of removing the mental obsession—is clear and makes sense to most compulsive eaters. The second is that it provides a powerful method of achieving recovery relatively quickly.

So if you're recovered, don't change what you're doing simply for the sake of change. If you haven't recovered, on the other hand, you owe it to yourself at least to consider the Big Book's approach. One thing is certain: if the Steps aren't working for you, then YOU aren't working the Steps! Find a way to work the Steps and you will recover!

Let me end with page 164 of the Big Book.

Just a note before quoting the passage. The second-last sentence has the word "trudge" in it. I know what some people say it means. They try to put a happy face on it. They say that "trudge" means " to walk with a determined pace". Not according to any good dictionary! No, it means what it sounds like—"to walk with a weary pace".

So we have our work cut out for us. The Big Book doesn't promise us a trouble-free life. As a matter of fact, it promises us a lot of work. There is a world of people dying from our illness, hopeless and despairing. We have a solution. Maybe it'll work for them. But it's hard work for us! So as we walk with a weary pace, as we do the hard work of carrying the message of recovery through the Twelve Steps, we are at least—and at last!—walking on a road which provides us with a happy destiny.

During our lives, and at the end of our lives, we will know that we have been useful to some other people. We will know that no matter what we have done in our lives and no matter what we have suffered in our lives, everything that has happened to us has been given meaning and has made us more fulfilled than we have ever been before. We will know that we can be changed into useful people. We will know what it means to be happy, joyous, and free! What a gift we have received! Let's give it away!

> Abandon yourself to God as you understand God. Admit your faults to Him and to your fellows. Clear away the wreckage of your past. Give freely of what you find and join us. We shall be with you in the Fellowship of the Spirit, and you will surely meet some of us as you trudge the Road of Happy Destiny. May God bless you and keep you—until then.

Appendices

Appendix One—Schematic Outline

Schematic Outline of the first 103 pages of the Big Book

I. The Doctor's Opinion

- A. First letter (xxiii–xxiv): You may rely absolutely on anything they say about themselves.
- B. The authors summarize the second letter (xxiv–xxv)—[T]he body of the alcoholic is quite as abnormal as his mind. . . . In our belief, any picture of the alcoholic which leaves out this physical factor is incomplete.
- C. Second letter (xxv–xxx): [T]hey cannot start drinking without developing the phenomenon of craving. This phenomenon, as we have suggested, may be the manifestation of an allergy which differentiates these people . . . .

II. Chapter 1: Bill's Story

- A. Alcohol is the high part of life (1–5)
- B. Alcohol becomes a necessity (5–7)
- C. The kind doctor explains the physical craving and the mental obsession; but self-knowledge doesn't work (7)
- D. Bill reaches the bottom—Bill's Step 1 (8)
- E. Ebby tells Bill about the religious solution and expands it to create the spiritual solution, open to all—Bill's Step 2 (9–12)
- F. Bill takes Steps 3 through 9 (13)
- G. Bill has a spiritual experience (14)
- H. Bill works Steps 10 through 12 (14–16)

III. Chapter 2: There is a Solution

- A. We have solved the drink problem and are united by a common solution (the Twelve Steps) (17)
- B. Alcoholism is an illness which has not been solved by professionals but alcoholics can be reached through fellow-suffers (18–19)
- C. This book is our attempt to provide the solution to all your problems by telling you what we did (19–20)
- D. The summary of the alcoholic problem:
  1. The physical craving overwhelms the alcoholic; once he starts drinking, he cannot stop (21–22)
  2. The mental obsession tells him that he does not have the physical reaction, so that he can go back to drinking even when sober: Therefore, the main problem of the alcoholic centers in his mind, rather than in his body. (22–25)
- E. There is a solution—deep and effective spiritual experiences which have revolutionized our whole attitude toward life, toward our fellows and toward God's universe. (25–26) (And note footnotes leading us to the Appendix on "Spiritual Experience", 569–570.)
- F. Rowland Hazard's encounter with Dr. Jung—spiritual experiences, or huge emotional displacements and rearrangements are necessary, but cannot usually be reached through religion for the true alcoholic (26–28)
- G. This book contains clear-cut directions . . . showing how we recovered. (28–29)

IV. Chapter 3: More about Alcoholism

- A. The mental obsession in general: The idea that somehow, someday he will control and enjoy his drinking is the great obsession of every abnormal drinker. (30)
- B. We must smash the delusion that we will ever become physically normal—the craving will always hit us if we drink alcohol (30–32)
  1. The man of thirty—his falling victim first, to the mental obsession, and then, to the physical craving, after twenty-five years of sobriety (32–33)
- C. Will-power is not sufficient for the alcoholic; we'll give examples so you can see whether you are an alcoholic (33–35)

1. Jim—the car salesman who had a bad day; who had knowledge about himself but gave it all up for the foolish idea that he could take whiskey if only he mixed it with milk! (35–37)
2. The jay-walker, who knows the danger but can't stop (37–39)
3. Fred—the accountant who had a good day; who had self-knowledge and knew the problem, but decided that it would be nice to have a couple of cocktails with dinner. (39–42)

D. Summary: The alcoholic at certain times has no effective mental defense against the first drink. Except in a few rare cases, neither he nor any other human being can provide such a defense. His defense must come from a Higher Power. (43)

V. Chapter 4: We Agnostics

A. We need a spiritual experience to conquer the illness; although this may appear to pose difficulties for the agnostic or atheist, don't worry (44)
B. Will-power isn't enough; we don't have enough power to overcome alcoholism: We had to find a power by which we could live, and it had to be a Power greater than ourselves. Obviously. But where and how were we to find this Power? Well, that's exactly what this book is about. Its main object is to enable you to find a Power greater than yourself which will solve your problem. (44–46)
C. All we need is willingness to believe (46–48)
D. Why believe in a Power greater than yourself? (48)
   1. Practically speaking, we believe in theories if they are grounded in fact—if they explain facts
      a. Our theory is that a spiritual experience solves our problem; and
      b. The fact is that we have solved our problem: the consciousness of the Presence of God is today the most important fact of [our] lives (48–51)
   2. Practically speaking, a willingness to change our belief system leads to being able to do things that are thought to be impossible (Galileo, the Wright brothers, our experience) (51–52)
   3. Clearly self-sufficiency and logic don't work as a theory (52–53)

E. The choice is clear: God either is, or He isn't. What was our choice to be? We are squarely confronted with the question of faith. (53)
   1. Faith is necessary to reach our solution (53)
   2. We already have some faith—in our reasoning, our ability to think (53–54)
   3. We are already worshippers, worshipping people, money, ourselves, the sunset, the sea, a flower; loving others (54)
   4. Everything really important to us has nothing to do with reason—it is all faith (54–55)

F. Deep down inside us is God; it may be obscured but the idea of God is there. He was as much a fact as we were. We found the Great Reality deep down within us. In the last analysis it is only there that He may be found. (55)
G. Fitz's story: "Our Southern Friend"—Who are you to say there is no God? (55–57)

VI. Chapter 5: How It Works

A. Our path works if we are honest; the way is hard and requires complete dedication; but you can draw on God's power to help you; and half measures will avail you nothing (58–59)
B. The Twelve Steps (59–60)
C. If we are convinced that we are alcoholic, that human power cannot relieve us, and that God can, then we're ready to take Step 3 (60)

D. Step 3
   1. Turn our will over to God: any life run on self-will can hardly be a success; we're like actors in a play who want to be the directors; we are selfish in that we want our way, whether it's for the worst or the best of reasons (60–62)
   2. Turn our life over to God: decide that hereafter in this drama of life, God was going to be our Director. (62–63)
   3. The promises as we take the steps—to have a new Employer (63)

4. The Step 3 prayer—to be taken with an understanding person (63)

E. Step 4—the beginning of our inventory—the fact-finding (searching) and fact-facing (fearless) examination of what is blocking us from the sunlight of the spirit; being convinced that our selfishness (self-centredness, self-pity, self-delusion, fear) is at the heart of our problem, we considered its common manifestations (63–64)
   1. Resentment—the Past did not go my way (64–67)—see form for details
   2. Fear—the Future won't go my way (67–68)—see form for details
   3. Sex Conduct—those relationships in which physical attraction was mixed in are the examples in our past by which we try to shape a sane and sound ideal for all relationships (68–70)—see form for details
   4. If we have written all this down, we have made an inventory of [our] grosser handicaps (71)

VII. Chapter 6: Into Action

A. Step 5
   1. Why we need to do Step 5
      a. We need objectivity to make certain that we know what has been blocking us from God (72)
      b. We have to be honest with another person (72–74)
   2. That person must be able to keep a confidence, understand and approve of what we're doing, and won't change our plan (74–76)
   3. Action of Step 5
      a. We must explain to that person why this is so important to us (75)
      b. We tell that person every twist of character, every dark cranny of the past (75)
      c. If we've been thorough, there are promises (75)
      d. We then go home and meditate, asking God whether we have omitted anything (75)

B. Step 6
   1. Are we ready to have God remove those things which are blocking us from God? (76)

C. Step 7
   1. The Step 7 prayer

D. Steps 8 and 9
   1. We have a list and we must remove those things which have blocked us by sweeping away the debris which has accumulated out of our effort to live on self-will and run the show ourselves. We have to do this (76–77)

   2. Direct Amends
      a. Making the amends when there is no harm done
         (1) Eyeball to eyeball (77–78)
         (2) Restitution (example of money) (78)
         (3) Taking consequences for our past actions (example of criminal offence) (78–79)
      b. Making the amends when harm may be done
         (1) Restitution (example of unpaid alimony and harm to new family) (79)
         (2) Taking consequences for our past actions (example of denial of loan and harm to partner and family) (80)
         (3) Eyeball to eyeball (example of infidelity and harm to the person to whom we make amends) (80–82)

   3. Living Amends—the period of reconstruction, where saying sorry isn't enough (82–83)
   4. Amends we cannot make; it's okay so long as we're ready to make them (83)
   5. The promises halfway through Step 9 (83–84)

E. Step 10
   1. The continuation of the inventory process—Steps 4 through 9—whenever needed (84)
   2. The promises at the end of Step 9 and the beginning of Step 10—Sanity is reached at last! We are neutral to alcohol—we no longer have the mental obsession (84–85)

F. Step 11
   1. Retiring at night—reviewing our day and doing an inventory process (Steps 4 through 9) in our meditation (86)
   2. Awakening in the morning—previewing our day and asking God to free us from self-will (86–87)
   3. As we go through the day—reminding ourselves we're no longer in charge (87–88)

VIII. Chapter 7: Working with Others

A. Step 12: carrying the message

B. Find a prospect, find out all you can, and see if he wants to see you (89–91)

C. First meeting
   1. Talk generally, lead into drinking stories, qualify (91)
   2. Describe self as an alcoholic, describe the physical craving and the mental obsession, and the hopelessness (91–92)
   3. Offer your solution, and explain the spiritual aspect of it (92–94)
   4. Outline the programme of action (94)
   5. Give him a copy of the Big Book and encourage him to read it, but don't spend much more time with him, and don't push him (94–96)

D. Second meeting
   1. If he wants to go through the Twelve Steps, sponsor him, offer to be with him in Step 3 and to hear his Step 5 (96)

E. Sponsorship
   1. Help him, but not at your expense and not in a way that makes him dependent upon you (96–98)
   2. Help his family, if you can (98–100)

F. Our freedom—what we can do—how we can be near alcohol with no problem, so long as we are spiritually fit (100–102)

G. Our job description: to be at the place where you may be of maximum helpfulness to others (102–103)

Appendix Two—Promises Checklist

A Big Book Checklist of Promises
(What step are you on?)

Steps One and Two:

- ► Is it clear to me that I am a compulsive overeater and cannot manage my own life?
- ► Is it clear that no human power can relieve my compulsive overeating?
- ► Is it clear that God can and will relieve my compulsive overeating if I seek God?

After Step Three:

- ► Was an effect, even a very great one, felt at once?

After Step Four:

- ► Have I written down a lot?
- ► Have I listed and analyzed my resentments?
- ► Have I begun to comprehend the futility and fatality of my resentments?
- ► Have I begun to learn tolerance, patience, and good will toward all men, even my enemies?
- ► Do I look on my enemies as sick people?
- ► Have I listed the people I hurt by my conduct and am I willing to straighten out the past if I can?
- ► Am I convinced that God can remove whatever self-will has blocked me off from Him?
- ► Have I swallowed and digested some big chunks of truth about myself?

After Step Five:

- ► Am I delighted?
- ► Can I look the world in the eye?
- ► Can I be alone at perfect peace and ease?
- ► Have my fears fallen from me?
- ► Have I begun to feel the nearness of my Creator?
- ► Am I beginning to have a spiritual experience?
- ► Has the eating problem disappeared (not always)?
- ► Do I feel as if I am on the Broad Highway, walking hand in hand with the Spirit of the Universe?
- ► Is my work solid so far?
- ► Are the stones properly in place? Have I skimped on the cement put into the foundation? Have I tried to make mortar without sand?

Before half-way through Step Nine (the Promises):

- ► Do I know a new freedom and a new happiness?
- ► Do I not regret the past nor wish to shut the door on it?
- ► Do I comprehend the word serenity and do I know peace?
- ► Do I see how my experience can benefit others, no matter how far down the scale I have gone?
- ► Has that feeling of uselessness and self-pity disappeared?
- ► Have I lost interest in selfish things and gained interested in my fellows?
- ► Has self-seeking slipped away?
- ► Has my whole attitude and outlook upon life changed?
- ► Has fear of people and of economic insecurity left me?
- ► Do I intuitively know how to handle situations which used to baffle me?
- ► Have I suddenly realized that God is doing for me what I could not do for myself?

After Step Nine:

- Have I ceased fighting anything or any one—even food?
- Has sanity returned?
- Am I seldom interested in food?
- If tempted by food, do I recoil from it as from a hot flame.
- Am I reacting sanely and normally, and has this happened automatically?
- Do I feel as though I had been placed in a position of neutrality, safe and protected?
- Has the problem been removed? Has it ceased to exist for me?
- Am I neither cocky nor afraid?

After Step Ten:

- Have I begun to sense the flow of His Spirit into me?
- Have I to some extent become God conscious? Have I begun to develop this vital sixth sense?

After Step Eleven:

- Am I surprised how the right answers have come when I have tried to relax, take it easy, and wait for God's inspiration, intuitive thought, or decision.
- Has what used to be the hunch or the occasional inspiration gradually become a working part of the mind?
- As time passes, is my thinking more and more on the plane of inspiration?
- Am I in much less danger of excitement, fear, anger, worry, self-pity, or foolish decisions?
- Have I become much more efficient?
- Do I not tire so easily?

After Step Twelve

- Has life taken on a new meaning?
- Do I not want to miss the opportunity to watch people recover, to see them help others, to watch loneliness vanish, to see a fellowship grow up about you, to have a host of friends?
- Have remarkable things happened?
- Am I presently living in a new and wonderful world, no matter what my present circumstances?
- Can I do all sorts of things compulsive eaters are not supposed to do?
- Can I go where my killer-food is served; can I have my killer-food in my home; do I see friends who eat my killer-food; do I watch movies or television which show scenes of eating my killer-food; do I go to restaurants which serve my killer-food; do my friends no longer have to hide their stores of killer-food when I visit them; can I be reminded of my killer-food?
- Have I found release from care, boredom and worry?
- Has my imagination been fired?
- Does life mean something at last?
- Do I know what it means to give of myself that others may survive and rediscover life?
- Have I learned the full meaning of "Love thy neighbor as thyself"?
- Has God shown me how to create the fellowship I crave?
- Have great events come to pass for me and countless others?

The Arch of Freedom

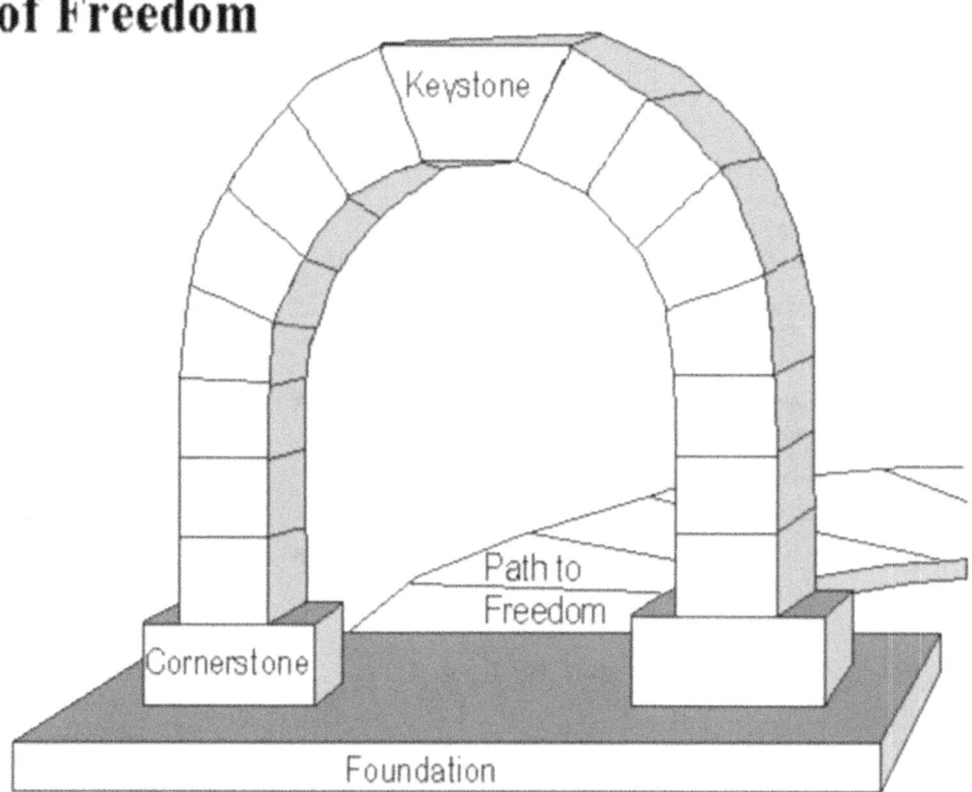

From Alcoholics Anonymous, the Big Book:

Foundation (page 12, Bill's Story): Step One -- Willingness through despair
It was only a matter of being willing to believe in a Power greater than myself. Nothing more way required of me to make my beginning. I saw that growth could start from that point. Upon a foundation of complete willingness I might build what I saw in my friend. Would I have it? Of course I would!

(page 25, There is a Solution)
There is a solution. Almost none of us liked the self-searching, the levelling of our pride, the confession of shortcomings which the process requires for its successful consummation. But we saw that it really worked in others, and we had come to believe in the hopelessness and futility of life as we had been living it. When, therefore, we were approached by those in whom the problem had been solved, there was nothing for us to do but pick up the simple kit of spiritual tools laid at our feet. We have found much of heaven and we have been rocketed into a fourth dimension of existence of which we had not even dreamed.

Cornerstone (page 47, We Agnostics): Step Two -- Belief through hope
We needed to ask ourselves but one short question. Do I now believe, or am I even willing to believe, that there is a Power greater than myself?" As soon as a man can say that he does believe, or is willing to believe, we emphatically assure him that he is on his way. It has been repeatedly proven among us that upon this simple cornerstone a wonderfully effective spiritual structure can be built. (Related to page 53 and the story on page 56, crossing from the Bridge of Reason to the shore of faith.)

Keystone (page 62, How it Works): Step Three -- Direction through decision
This is the how and why of it. First of all, we had to quit playing God. It didn't work. Next, we decided that hereafter in this drama of life, God was going to be our Director. He is the Principal; we are his agents. He is the Father, and we are His children. Most good ideas are simple, and this concept was the keystone of the new and triumphant arch through which we passed to freedom.

Path (page 75, Into Action): Steps Four through Nine -- Freedom through action
Carefully reading the first five proposals we ask ourselves if we have omitted anything, for we are building an arch through which we shall walk a free man at last. Is our work solid so far? Are the stones properly in place? Have we skimped on the cement put into the foundation? Have we tried to make mortar without sand?

What follows are some examples of how someone might fill out the Step Four forms. There will usually be many more resentments and fears. These are only intended as examples of different kinds of resentments in order to show how the forms might be filled in.

Clear Form

The "BIG BOOK'S" Way to Be Rid of Resentment (pages 63—67)

INSTRUCTIONS: **Study** from the bottom of page 63 to the end of page 65 and **then** follow its instructions: a) List all people, institutions and principles (Column 1) from **top to bottom**. b) List all "causes" (Column 2), **top to bottom**. c) Do all six instincts in Column 3 from **top to bottom for each "cause"**. d) Consider the first three columns carefully. e) Then, complete Column 4 from **top to bottom.**

DON'T FORGET THIS! **Study** from the bottom of page 65 to end of the 3rd paragraph on page 67, and **then** follow the instructions. Go to each person who has harmed you or someone and say "_____ is spiritually sick." Don't forget to say the Resentment Prayer (Lines 3-5, page 67), "God, please help me show _____ the same tolerance, pity and patience I would cheerfully grant a sick friend" for each and every person who has harmed you, themselves or someone else in Column 1 prior to starting Column 4.

Core Character Defects (4): "Putting out of our minds the wrongs others have done, **[use fold lines to cover Columns 2 and 3]** we resolutely looked for our own mistakes. Where had we been selfish, dishonest, self-seeking and frightened? . . . [D]isregard the other person involved entirely. Where were we to blame? . . . When we saw our faults we **listed** them. We placed them before us in **black and white.** We admitted our wrongs honestly and were willing to set these matters straight." (page 67)

I'm resentful at: (1)	The causes: (2)	Self-Esteem	Security (Pkt. Books)	Ambitions	Personal Relations	Sex Relations	Is any fear involved?	Core Character Defects (4)
I'll never be thin								Selfish:
								Dishonest:
								Self-Seeking:
								Frightened:
I did this in AA – why should I do this in OA?								Selfish:
								Dishonest:
								Self-Seeking:
								Frightened:
People are suffering terribly in this world								Selfish:
								Dishonest:
								Self-Seeking:
								Frightened:

Clear Form

The "BIG BOOK'S" Way to Be Rid of Resentment (pages 63—67)

INSTRUCTIONS: **Study** from the bottom of page 63 to the end of page 65 and **then** follow its instructions: a) List all people, institutions and principles (Column 1) from **top to bottom**. b) List all "causes" (Column 2), **top to bottom**. c) Do all six instincts in Column 3 from **top to bottom for each "cause"**. d) Consider the first three columns carefully. e) Then, complete Column 4 from **top to bottom.**

DON'T FORGET THIS! **Study** from the bottom of page 65 to end of the 3rd paragraph on page 67, and **then** follow the instructions. Go to each person who has harmed you or someone and say "_____ is spiritually sick." Don't forget to say the Resentment Prayer (Lines 3-5, page 67), "God, please help me show _____ the same tolerance, pity and patience I would cheerfully grant a sick friend" for each and every person who has harmed you, themselves or someone else in Column 1 prior to starting Column 4.

Core Character Defects (4): "Putting out of our minds the wrongs others have done, **[use fold lines to cover Columns 2 and 3]** we resolutely looked for our own mistakes. Where had we been selfish, dishonest, self-seeking and frightened? . . . [D]isregard the other person involved entirely. Where were we to blame? . . . When we saw our faults we **listed** them. We placed them before us in **black and white.** We admitted our wrongs honestly and were willing to set these matters straight." (page 67)

I'm resentful at: (1)	The causes: (2)	Self-Esteem	Security (Pkt. Books)	Ambitions	Personal Relations	Sex Relations	Is any fear involved?	Core Character Defects (4)
spouse								Selfish:
								Dishonest:
								Self-Seeking:
								Frightened:
person who hurt me								Selfish:
								Dishonest:
								Self-Seeking:
								Frightened:
people who don't park within the lines								Selfish:
								Dishonest:
								Self-Seeking:
								Frightened:

Clear Form

The "BIG BOOK'S" Way to Be Rid of Resentment (pages 63—67)

INSTRUCTIONS: **Study** from the bottom of page 63 to the end of page 65 and **then** follow its instructions: a) List all people, institutions and principles (Column 1) from **top to bottom**. b) List all "causes" (Column 2), **top to bottom**. c) Do all six instincts in Column 3 from **top to bottom for each "cause"**. d) Consider the first three columns carefully. e) Then, complete Column 4 from **top to bottom.**

DON'T FORGET THIS! **Study** from the bottom of page 65 to end of the 3rd paragraph on page 67, and **then** follow the instructions. Go to each person who has harmed you or someone and say "_____ is spiritually sick." Don't forget to say the Resentment Prayer (Lines 3-5, page 67), "God, please help me show _____ the same tolerance, pity and patience I would cheerfully grant a sick friend" for each and every person who has harmed you, themselves or someone else in Column 1 prior to starting Column 4.

Core Character Defects (4): "Putting out of our minds the wrongs others have done, **[use fold lines to cover Columns 2 and 3]** we resolutely looked for our own mistakes. Where had we been selfish, dishonest, self-seeking and frightened? . . . [D]isregard the other person involved entirely. Where were we to blame? . . . When we saw our faults we **listed** them. We placed them before us in **black and white.** We admitted our wrongs honestly and were willing to set these matters straight." (page 67)

I'm resentful at: (1)	The causes: (2)	Self-Esteem	Security (Pkt. Books)	Ambitions	Personal Relations	Sex Relations	Is any fear involved?	Core Character Defects (4)
I'll never be thin	I always start off enthusiastically,							Selfish:
	and then fail.							
	I don't have faith in this program.							Dishonest:
	I don't have the right sponsor.							
	I always screw up.							Self-Seeking:
	I hate being fat!							
								Frightened:
I did this in AA – why should I do this in OA?	AA is much more important to me.							Selfish:
	AA has much more recovery.							
	I know more than my sponsor does							Dishonest:
	about the Twelve Steps.							
								Self-Seeking:
								Frightened:
People are suffering terribly in this world	I'm enjoying my life and other							Selfish:
	people are dying.							
	I am powerless over the horrible							Dishonest:
	things that are going on.							
	Things have to change for the							Self-Seeking:
	better!							
								Frightened:

Clear Form

The "BIG BOOK'S" Way to Be Rid of Resentment (pages 63—67)

INSTRUCTIONS: **Study** from the bottom of page 63 to the end of page 65 and **then** follow its instructions: a) List all people, institutions and principles (Column 1) from **top to bottom**. b) List all "causes" (Column 2), **top to bottom**. c) Do all six instincts in Column 3 from **top to bottom for each "cause"**. d) Consider the first three columns carefully. e) Then, complete Column 4 from **top to bottom.**

DON'T FORGET THIS! **Study** from the bottom of page 65 to end of the 3rd paragraph on page 67, and **then** follow the instructions. Go to each person who has harmed you or someone and say "_____ is spiritually sick." Don't forget to say the Resentment Prayer (Lines 3-5, page 67), "God, please help me show _____ the same tolerance, pity and patience I would cheerfully grant a sick friend" for each and every person who has harmed you, themselves or someone else in Column 1 prior to starting Column 4.

Core Character Defects (4): "Putting out of our minds the wrongs others have done, **[use fold lines to cover Columns 2 and 3]** we resolutely looked for our own mistakes. Where had we been selfish, dishonest, self-seeking and frightened? . . . [D]isregard the other person involved entirely. Where were we to blame? . . . When we saw our faults we **listed** them. We placed them before us in **black and white.** We admitted our wrongs honestly and were willing to set these matters straight." (page 67)

I'm resentful at: (1)	The causes: (2)	Self-Esteem	Security (Pkt. Books)	Ambitions	Personal Relations	Sex Relations	Is any fear involved?	Core Character Defects (4)
spouse	not enough sex							Selfish:
	doesn't help around the house							
	isn't supportive of me in OA							Dishonest:
	full of anger							
	spends too much money on self							Self-Seeking:
	doesn't do part in parenting							
	calls me fat							Frightened:
person who hurt me as a child	betrayed my trust							Selfish:
	caused me physical pain							
	caused me emotional pain							Dishonest:
	continues to make me feel terrible							
	changed my life completely							Self-Seeking:
	made me into a loser							
	I think of that person all the time							Frightened:
	I am full of hatred							
	I am full of self-pity							
people who don't park within the lines	don't care about others							Selfish:
	only interested in themselves							
	forced me to walk a block							Dishonest:
	I got angry and yelled at my kids							
	later							Self-Seeking:
								Frightened:

Clear Form

The "BIG BOOK'S" Way to Be Rid of Resentment (pages 63—67)

INSTRUCTIONS: **Study** from the bottom of page 63 to the end of page 65 and **then** follow its instructions: a) List all people, institutions and principles (Column 1) from **top to bottom**. b) List all "causes" (Column 2), **top to bottom**. c) Do all six instincts in Column 3 from **top to bottom for each "cause"**. d) Consider the first three columns carefully. e) Then, complete Column 4 from **top to bottom.**

DON'T FORGET THIS! **Study** from the bottom of page 65 to end of the 3rd paragraph on page 67, and **then** follow the instructions. Go to *each person who has harmed you or someone and say "____ is spiritually sick." Don't forget to say the Resentment Prayer (Lines 3-5, page 67), "God, please help me show ____ the same tolerance, pity and patience I would cheerfully grant a sick friend" for each and every person who has harmed you, themselves or someone else in Column 1 prior to starting Column 4.*

Core Character Defects (4): "Putting out of our minds the wrongs others have done, **[use fold lines to cover Columns 2 and 3]** we resolutely looked for our own mistakes. Where had we been selfish, dishonest, self-seeking and frightened? . . . [D]isregard the other person involved entirely. Where were we to blame? . . . When we saw our faults we **listed** them. We placed them before us in **black and white**. We admitted our wrongs honestly and were willing to set these matters straight." (page 67)

I'm resentful at: (1)	The causes: (2)	Self-Esteem	Security (Pkt. Books)	Ambitions	Personal Relations	Sex Relations	Is any fear involved?	Core Character Defects (4)
I'll never be thin	I always start off enthusiastically,	✔	✔	✔	✔		✔	**Selfish:**
	and then fail.							**Dishonest:**
	I don't have faith in this program.		✔	✔			✔	**Self-Seeking:**
	I don't have the right sponsor.	✔	✔	✔	✔		✔	**Frightened:**
	I always screw up.	✔	✔	✔	✔	✔	✔	
	I hate being fat!	✔	✔	✔	✔	✔	✔	
I did this in AA -- why should I do this in OA?	AA is much more important to me.			✔			✔	**Selfish:**
	AA has much more recovery.		✔	✔			✔	**Dishonest:**
	I know more than my sponsor does	✔	✔	✔	✔		✔	**Self-Seeking:**
	about the Twelve Steps.							**Frightened:**
People are suffering terribly in this world	I'm enjoying my life and other		✔	✔			✔	**Selfish:**
	people are dying.							**Dishonest:**
	I am powerless over the horrible	✔	✔	✔			✔	**Self-Seeking:**
	things that are going on.							**Frightened:**
	Things have to change for the		✔	✔			✔	
	better!							

Clear Form

The "BIG BOOK'S" Way to Be Rid of Resentment (pages 63—67)

INSTRUCTIONS: **Study** from the bottom of page 63 to the end of page 65 and **then** follow its instructions: a) List all people, institutions and principles (Column 1) from **top to bottom**. b) List all "causes" (Column 2), **top to bottom**. c) Do all six instincts in Column 3 from **top to bottom for each "cause"**. d) Consider the first three columns carefully. e) Then, complete Column 4 from **top to bottom.**

DON'T FORGET THIS! **Study** from the bottom of page 65 to end of the 3rd paragraph on page 67, and **then** follow the instructions. Go to *each person who has harmed you or someone and say "____ is spiritually sick." Don't forget to say the Resentment Prayer (Lines 3-5, page 67), "God, please help me show ____ the same tolerance, pity and patience I would cheerfully grant a sick friend" for each and every person who has harmed you, themselves or someone else in Column 1 prior to starting Column 4.*

Core Character Defects (4): "Putting out of our minds the wrongs others have done, **[use fold lines to cover Columns 2 and 3]** we resolutely looked for our own mistakes. Where had we been selfish, dishonest, self-seeking and frightened? . . . [D]isregard the other person involved entirely. Where were we to blame? . . . When we saw our faults we **listed** them. We placed them before us in **black and white**. We admitted our wrongs honestly and were willing to set these matters straight." (page 67)

I'm resentful at: (1)	The causes: (2)	Self-Esteem	Security (Pkt. Books)	Ambitions	Personal Relations	Sex Relations	Is any fear involved?	Core Character Defects (4)
spouse	not enough sex	✔		✔	✔	✔	✔	**Selfish:**
	doesn't help around the house	✔	✔	✔	✔	✔	✔	**Dishonest:**
	isn't supportive of me in OA	✔	✔	✔	✔		✔	**Self-Seeking:**
	full of anger		✔	✔	✔	✔	✔	**Frightened:**
	spends too much money on self	✔	✔	✔			✔	
	doesn't do part in parenting		✔	✔			✔	
	calls me fat	✔		✔	✔	✔	✔	
person who hurt me as a child	betrayed my trust	✔	✔	✔	✔	✔	✔	**Selfish:**
	caused me physical pain		✔	✔	✔	✔		**Dishonest:**
	caused me emotional pain	✔	✔	✔	✔	✔	✔	**Self-Seeking:**
	continues to make me feel terrible	✔	✔	✔	✔	✔	✔	**Frightened:**
	changed my life completely	✔	✔	✔	✔	✔	✔	
	made me into a loser	✔	✔	✔	✔	✔	✔	
	I think of that person all the time	✔	✔	✔		✔	✔	
	I am full of hatred	✔	✔	✔	✔	✔	✔	
	I am full of self-pity	✔	✔	✔	✔	✔	✔	
people who don't park within the lines	don't care about others			✔			✔	**Selfish:**
	only interested in themselves			✔			✔	**Dishonest:**
	forced me to walk a block	✔		✔			✔	**Self-Seeking:**
	I got angry and yelled at my kids	✔		✔	✔		✔	**Frightened:**
	later							

Clear Form

The "BIG BOOK'S" Way to Be Rid of Resentment (pages 63—67)

INSTRUCTIONS: **Study** from the bottom of page 63 to the end of page 65 and **then** follow its instructions: a) List all people, institutions and principles (Column 1) from **top to bottom**. b) List all "causes" (Column 2), **top to bottom**. c) Do all six instincts in Column 3 from **top to bottom for each "cause"**. d) Consider the first three columns carefully. e) Then, complete Column 4 from **top to bottom.**

DON'T FORGET THIS! **Study** from the bottom of page 65 to end of the 3rd paragraph on page 67, and **then** follow the instructions. Go to *each person who has harmed you or someone and say "____ is spiritually sick." Don't forget to say the Resentment Prayer (Lines 3-5, page 67), "God, please help me show ____ the same tolerance, pity and patience I would cheerfully grant a sick friend" for each and every person who has harmed you, themselves or someone else in Column 1 prior to starting Column 4.*

Core Character Defects (4): "Putting out of our minds the wrongs others have done, **[use fold lines to cover Columns 2 and 3]** we resolutely looked for our own mistakes. Where had we been selfish, dishonest, self-seeking and frightened? . . . [D]isregard the other person involved entirely. Where were we to blame? . . . When we saw our faults we **listed** them. We placed them before us in **black and white**. We admitted our wrongs honestly and were willing to set these matters straight." (page 67)

I'm resentful at: (1)	The causes: (2)	Self-Esteem	Security (Pkt. Books)	Ambitions	Personal Relations	Sex Relations	Is any fear involved?	Core Character Defects (4)
I'll never be thin	I always start off enthusiastically,	✔	✔	✔	✔		✔	**Selfish:** I want to be thin my own way. Want it to be easy.
	and then fail.							**Dishonest:** There's a part of me that feels more comfortable being fat. I always undermine myself. I've never taken this seriously. I don't want to be a sex object.
	I don't have faith in this program.		✔	✔			✔	**Self-Seeking:** I want to be a sex object! I want to attract people. I feel stupid and awful and victimized the way I am.
	I don't have the right sponsor.	✔	✔	✔	✔		✔	**Frightened:** That nothing will change.
	I always screw up.	✔	✔	✔	✔	✔	✔	
	I hate being fat!	✔	✔	✔	✔	✔	✔	
I did this in AA -- why should I do this in OA?	AA is much more important to me.			✔			✔	**Selfish:** I was comfortable in AA. I don't want to be uncomfortable. I don't want to do any more work than what I do now.
	AA has much more recovery.		✔	✔			✔	**Dishonest:** If AA were going to do the job, it would have done the job. I have not found a Higher Power that restored my sanity when it comes to my compulsive eating.
	I know more than my sponsor does	✔	✔	✔	✔		✔	**Self-Seeking:** I'm in the grand-daddy of all the programs, and I have to lower myself to be in this one?
	about the Twelve Steps.							**Frightened:** That I'll never get thin; that I'll never find freedom from the bondage of food.
People are suffering terribly in this world	I'm enjoying my life and other		✔	✔			✔	**Selfish:** I want things to happen for the good for all people.
	people are dying.							**Dishonest:** I am indeed powerless over the fate of millions of other people. I waste my energies that could be used for good by spending my time thinking about things I can't do.
	I am powerless over the horrible	✔	✔	✔			✔	**Self-Seeking:** If I were in charge of the world, life would be better for everybody!
	things that are going on.							**Frightened:** That nothing will change.
	Things have to change for the		✔	✔			✔	
	better!							

Clear Form

The "BIG BOOK'S" Way to Be Rid of Resentment (pages 63—67)

INSTRUCTIONS: **Study** from the bottom of page 63 to the end of page 65 and **then** follow its instructions: a) List all people, institutions and principles (Column 1) from **top to bottom**. b) List all "causes" (Column 2), **top to bottom**. c) Do all six instincts in Column 3 from **top to bottom for each "cause"**. d) Consider the first three columns carefully. e) Then, complete Column 4 from **top to bottom.**

DON'T FORGET THIS! **Study** from the bottom of page 65 to end of the 3rd paragraph on page 67, and **then** follow the instructions. Go to *each person who has harmed you or someone and say "____ is spiritually sick." Don't forget to say the Resentment Prayer (Lines 3-5, page 67), "God, please help me show ____ the same tolerance, pity and patience I would cheerfully grant a sick friend" for each and every person who has harmed you, themselves or someone else in Column 1 prior to starting Column 4.*

Core Character Defects (4): "Putting out of our minds the wrongs others have done, **[use fold lines to cover Columns 2 and 3]** we resolutely looked for our own mistakes. Where had we been selfish, dishonest, self-seeking and frightened? . . . [D]isregard the other person involved entirely. Where were we to blame? . . . When we saw our faults we **listed** them. We placed them before us in **black and white**. We admitted our wrongs honestly and were willing to set these matters straight." (page 67)

I'm resentful at: (1)	The causes: (2)	Self-Esteem	Security (Pkt. Books)	Ambitions	Personal Relations	Sex Relations	Is any fear involved?	Core Character Defects (4)
spouse	not enough sex	✔		✔	✔	✔	✔	**Selfish:** want spouse to be different from what spouse is capable of right now; want my own way; want to feel safe; want to be loved; want partner to be good parent; want the partner of my childhood dreams
	doesn't help around the house	✔	✔	✔	✔	✔	✔	**Dishonest:** I can't change spouse; I married whom I married; I don't always tell spouse the truth that should be told about my own needs and wants; spouse has many great qualities which I should acknowledge. I love spouse.
	isn't supportive of me in OA	✔	✔	✔	✔		✔	**Self-Seeking:** There are times spouse makes me feel bad about myself. The relationship seems to be about me rather than about OUR relationship.
	full of anger		✔	✔	✔	✔	✔	**Frightened:** I'm afraid I may lose the relationship. I'm afraid of living alone. I'm afraid of raising the children by myself. I'm afraid of dating again. I'm afraid of being lonely.
	spends too much money on self	✔	✔	✔			✔	
	doesn't do part in parenting		✔	✔			✔	
	calls me fat	✔		✔	✔	✔	✔	
person who hurt me as a child	betrayed my trust	✔	✔	✔	✔	✔	✔	**Selfish:** I want the past not to have happened. I want to have had a relatively painless childhood. I want to have had a protected childhood. I want my life to have been different.
	caused me physical pain		✔	✔	✔	✔		**Dishonest:** What happened to me happened forty years ago. I can't change the past. I didn't tell the truth when it happened and I haven't told the truth to a number of people who should have known.
	caused me emotional pain	✔	✔	✔	✔	✔	✔	**Self-Seeking:** This changed how I felt and still feel about myself. I have felt damaged my whole life.
	continues to make me feel terrible	✔	✔	✔	✔	✔	✔	**Frightened:** Of trusting people, even those who love me. Of trusting myself. Of feeling this way for the rest of my life.
	changed my life completely	✔	✔	✔	✔	✔	✔	
	made me into a loser	✔	✔	✔	✔	✔	✔	
	I think of that person all the time	✔	✔	✔		✔	✔	
	I am full of hatred	✔	✔	✔	✔	✔	✔	
	I am full of self-pity	✔	✔	✔	✔	✔	✔	
people who don't park within the lines	don't care about others			✔			✔	**Selfish:** People should think of other people's discomfort.
	only interested in themselves			✔			✔	**Dishonest:** I've sometimes done it and thought I had good reason (in a hurry) not to correct it.
	forced me to walk a block	✔		✔			✔	**Self-Seeking:** I didn't deserve having it happen to me!
								Frightened: That something like this could get me so angry I would yell at my kids.

Clear Form

THE BIG BOOK'S WAY OF REMOVING FEARS (PP. 67 & 68)

INSTRUCTIONS: **a)** Study from the bottom of page 67 to the bottom of page 68 in the book *Alcoholics Anonymous.* **b)** Complete column 1 (listing whom or what I am fearful of), **from top to bottom**. **c)** Complete the remaining columns from **top to bottom** for each fear in column 1. Remember that "we are now on a different basis; the basis of trusting and relying upon God. We trust infinite God rather than our finite selves. . . . Just to the extent that we do as we think He would have us, and humbly rely on Him, does He enable us to match calamity with serenity" (page 68).

I'm fearful of: (1)	Why do I have the fear? (2)	Where was my trust & reliance? (3)	Did self reliance work? (4)	Fear Prayer: "God, please remove my fear and direct my attention to what you would have me be" (5)	What would God have you be? Write out your answer to that question for each and every fear listed. (6)
		Infinite God / My Finite Self	Yes / No	COMPLETED FEAR PRAYER? ☐	
My spouse	I'll lose her I'll never find anyone else I'll be alone all my life I'll have to raise the children myself	Infinite God / My Finite Self	Yes / No	COMPLETED FEAR PRAYER? ☐	
person who hurt me as a child	I'll never be over this hurt I won't be able to trust anyone My hating will cause me to eat I can't really enjoy sex or love	Infinite God / My Finite Self	Yes / No	COMPLETED FEAR PRAYER? ☐	
my kids	I'll yell at them I'll hurt them they'll die before me they'll hate me	Infinite God / My Finite Self	Yes / No	COMPLETED FEAR PRAYER? ☐	my kids
people will suffer in this world	I'll never be able to be happy I won't be able to help anyone It will get worse	Infinite God / My Finite Self	Yes / No	COMPLETED FEAR PRAYER? ☐	people will suffer in this world
I'll never be thin	I'll die early and painfully I'll never be attractive I won't be able to do the things I want to do in my life	Infinite God / My Finite Self	Yes / No	COMPLETED FEAR PRAYER? ☐	I'll never be thin
I'm going to die	It will be painful and slow I won't know what happens after	Infinite God / My Finite Self	Yes / No	COMPLETED FEAR PRAYER? ☐	I'm going to die
		Infinite God / My Finite Self	Yes / No	COMPLETED FEAR PRAYER? ☐	

Clear Form

THE BIG BOOK'S WAY OF REMOVING FEARS (PP. 67 & 68)

INSTRUCTIONS: **a)** Study from the bottom of page 67 to the bottom of page 68 in the book *Alcoholics Anonymous.* **b)** Complete column 1 (listing whom or what I am fearful of), **from top to bottom**. **c)** Complete the remaining columns from **top to bottom** for each fear in column 1. Remember that "we are now on a different basis; the basis of trusting and relying upon God. We trust infinite God rather than our finite selves. . . . Just to the extent that we do as we think He would have us, and humbly rely on Him, does He enable us to match calamity with serenity" (page 68).

I'm fearful of: (1)	Why do I have the fear? (2)	Where was my trust & reliance? (3)	Did self reliance work? (4)	Fear Prayer: "God, please remove my fear and direct my attention to what you would have me be" (5)	What would God have you be? Write out your answer to that question for each and every fear listed. (6)
				COMPLETED FEAR PRAYER? ☐	
My spouse				COMPLETED FEAR PRAYER? ☐	
person who hurt me as a child				COMPLETED FEAR PRAYER? ☐	
	my kids			COMPLETED FEAR PRAYER? ☐	my kids
	people will suffer in this world			COMPLETED FEAR PRAYER? ☐	people will suffer in this world
	I'll never be thin			COMPLETED FEAR PRAYER? ☐	I'll never be thin
	I'm going to die			COMPLETED FEAR PRAYER? ☐	I'm going to die
				COMPLETED FEAR PRAYER? ☐	

Clear Form

THE BIG BOOK'S WAY OF REMOVING FEARS (PP. 67 & 68)

INSTRUCTIONS: **a)** Study from the bottom of page 67 to the bottom of page 68 in the book *Alcoholics Anonymous.* **b)** Complete column 1 (listing whom or what I am fearful of), **from top to bottom**. **c)** Complete the remaining columns from **top to bottom** for each fear in column 1. Remember that "we are now on a different basis; the basis of trusting and relying upon God. We trust infinite God rather than our finite selves. . . . Just to the extent that we do as we think He would have us, and humbly rely on Him, does He enable us to match calamity with serenity" (page 68).

I'm fearful of: (1)	Why do I have the fear? (2)	Where was my trust & reliance? (3)	Did self reliance work? (4)	Fear Prayer: "God, please remove my fear and direct my attention to what you would have me be" (5)	What would God have you be? Write out your answer to that question for each and every fear listed. (6)
		Infinite God / **My Finite Self**	~~Yes~~ / (No)	COMPLETED FEAR PRAYER? ☐	
My spouse	I'll lose her I'll never find anyone else I'll be alone all my life I'll have to raise the children myself	Infinite God / **My Finite Self**	~~Yes~~ / (No)	COMPLETED FEAR PRAYER? ✔	A loving, compassionate, understanding, honest, giving person who thinks of my spouse more than me and who invests in our relationship together
person who hurt me as a child	I'll never be over this hurt I won't be able to trust anyone My hating will cause me to eat I can't really enjoy sex or love	Infinite God / **My Finite Self**	~~Yes~~ / (No)	COMPLETED FEAR PRAYER? ✔	A person who is free from hate, regret, fear, who can trust and enjoy life, who does not live in the past, who does not deny love to others
my kids	I'll yell at them I'll hurt them they'll die before me they'll hate me	Infinite God / **My Finite Self**	~~Yes~~ / (No)	COMPLETED FEAR PRAYER? ✔	A loving, compassionate, understanding, honest, giving parent who thinks of my children more than me and who invests in our relationship with each other
people will suffer in this world	I'll never be able to be happy I won't be able to help anyone It will get worse	Infinite God / **My Finite Self**	~~Yes~~ / (No)	COMPLETED FEAR PRAYER? ✔	A person who tries to help others and who is not paralyzed by what cannot be done and who is able to enjoy life on life's terms and accept happiness when happiness comes my way
I'll never be thin	I'll die early and painfully I'll never be attractive I won't be able to do the things I want to do in my life	Infinite God / **My Finite Self**	~~Yes~~ / (No)	COMPLETED FEAR PRAYER? ✔	A person who seeks a spiritual awakening to relieve me of my mental obsession so that I can remain abstinent and reach and maintain a healthy body weight
I'm going to die	It will be painful and slow I won't know what happens after	Infinite God / **My Finite Self**	~~Yes~~ / (No)	COMPLETED FEAR PRAYER? ✔	A person who keeps as healthy as I can and accepts that life is relatively short and gives of myself so that others may enjoy themselves.
		Infinite God / My Finite Self	Yes / No	COMPLETED FEAR PRAYER? ☐	

Clear Form

THE BIG BOOK'S WAY OF REMOVING FEARS (PP. 67 & 68)

INSTRUCTIONS: **a)** Study from the bottom of page 67 to the bottom of page 68 in the book *Alcoholics Anonymous.* **b)** Complete column 1 (listing whom or what I am fearful of), **from top to bottom**. **c)** Complete the remaining columns from **top to bottom** for each fear in column 1. Remember that "we are now on a different basis; the basis of trusting and relying upon God. We trust infinite God rather than our finite selves. . . . Just to the extent that we do as we think He would have us, and humbly rely on Him, does He enable us to match calamity with serenity" (page 68).

I'm fearful of: (1)	Why do I have the fear? (2)	Where was my trust & reliance? (3)	Did self reliance work? (4)	Fear Prayer: "God, please remove my fear and direct my attention to what you would have me be" (5)	What would God have you be? Write out your answer to that question for each and every fear listed. (6)
		Infinite God / **My Finite Self**	~~Yes~~ / (No)	COMPLETED FEAR PRAYER? ☐	
My spouse	I'll lose her I'll never find anyone else I'll be alone all my life I'll have to raise the children myself	Infinite God / **My Finite Self**	~~Yes~~ / (No)	COMPLETED FEAR PRAYER? ✔	
person who hurt me as a child	I'll never be over this hurt I won't be able to trust anyone My hating will cause me to eat I can't really enjoy sex or love	Infinite God / **My Finite Self**	~~Yes~~ / (No)	COMPLETED FEAR PRAYER? ✔	
my kids	I'll yell at them I'll hurt them they'll die before me they'll hate me	Infinite God / **My Finite Self**	~~Yes~~ / (No)	COMPLETED FEAR PRAYER? ✔	my kids
people will suffer in this world	I'll never be able to be happy I won't be able to help anyone It will get worse	Infinite God / **My Finite Self**	~~Yes~~ / (No)	COMPLETED FEAR PRAYER? ✔	people will suffer in this world
I'll never be thin	I'll die early and painfully I'll never be attractive I won't be able to do the things I want to do in my life	Infinite God / **My Finite Self**	~~Yes~~ / (No)	COMPLETED FEAR PRAYER? ✔	I'll never be thin
I'm going to die	It will be painful and slow I won't know what happens after	Infinite God / **My Finite Self**	~~Yes~~ / (No)	COMPLETED FEAR PRAYER? ✔	I'm going to die
		Infinite God / My Finite Self	Yes / No	COMPLETED FEAR PRAYER? ☐	

THE BIG BOOK'S WAY TO "SENSIBLY OVERHAUL" OUR OWN SEX CONDUCT (Pages 68—70)

INSTRUCTIONS: a) Study from the bottom of page 68 to the end of third paragraph on page 70. **b)** Fill in Column 1from top to bottom. **c)** Do Column 2 **from top to bottom. d)** Fill in each of the remaining columns **from top to bottom.** *Do not work across the page from left to right.* Don't forget the **Sex Prayer** ("God, please mold my ideals and help me to live up to them") on page 69, and the Big Book's **Sex Meditation** ("God, please show me what to do about this [each] specific matter") on page 69. "The right answer will come if we want it". This will shape a "sane and sound ideal for our future sex life" (page 69). Be sure to restudy what happens if we "fall short of the chosen ideal and stumble" on page 70. Be sure to continue to pray the "Earnest" prayers from page 70 (on the right hand side of this page) for ongoing guidance, strength, sanity, and the right ideal. **Clear Form Data**

Whom did I hurt? (1)	Where was I (2)	Did I arouse: (3)	Where was I at fault, what should I have done instead? (4)	Was each relation? (5)	Sex Prayer Page 69(6)	Sex Meditation Page 69(7)	The Earnest Prayers page 70
my spouse	Selfish: wanted spouse to be different; want my way; want sex; want love Dishonest: can't change anyone but myself; made choice; haven't been honest about needs and problems; haven't love what there is to love Inconsiderate: thought of myself and not spouse; how spouse feels affects how I feel about myself	Jealousy? Suspicion? Bitterness?		S E L F I S H Yes No	*"God, please mold my ideals and help me to live up to them."* ☐	*"God, please show me what to do about this[each] specific matter"* ☐	We earnestly pray for: The right ideal Guidance in each questionable situation
my ex	Selfish: wanted what I wanted from the relationship; ate myself out of the relationships thought of myself only; denied sex because of anger Dishonest: blamed spouse for the bad relationship instead of myself; did not invest myself into relationship; denied sex Inconsiderate: thought only of myself; thought I could fix things; didn't think of ex's needs or desires	Jealousy? Suspicion? Bitterness?		S E L F I S H Yes No	*"God, please mold my ideals and help me to live up to them."* ☐	*"God, please show me what to do about this[each] specific matter"* ☐	Sanity The strength to do the right thing If sex is troublesome, we throw ourselves the harder into helping others.
my high school sweetheart	Selfish: wanted sex without committed relationship; thought only of my needs; used other to get peer respect Dishonest: did not tell sweetheart the truth; lied about other relationships; pretended to be interested in things just to get the relationship Inconsiderate: my sexual needs were foremost; used the other in many ways	Jealousy? Suspicion? Bitterness?		S E L F I S H Yes No	*"God, please mold my ideals and help me to live up to them."* ☐	*"God, please show me what to do about this[each] specific matter"* ☐	We think of their needs and work for them. This takes us out of ourselves. It quiets the imperious urge, when to yield would mean heartache.

THE BIG BOOK'S WAY TO "SENSIBLY OVERHAUL" OUR OWN SEX CONDUCT (Pages 68—70)

INSTRUCTIONS: a) Study from the bottom of page 68 to the end of third paragraph on page 70. **b)** Fill in Column 1from top to bottom. **c)** Do Column 2 **from top to bottom. d)** Fill in each of the remaining columns **from top to bottom.** *Do not work across the page from left to right.* Don't forget the **Sex Prayer** ("God, please mold my ideals and help me to live up to them") on page 69, and the Big Book's **Sex Meditation** ("God, please show me what to do about this [each] specific matter") on page 69. "The right answer will come if we want it". This will shape a "sane and sound ideal for our future sex life" (page 69). Be sure to restudy what happens if we "fall short of the chosen ideal and stumble" on page 70. Be sure to continue to pray the "Earnest" prayers from page 70 (on the right hand side of this page) for ongoing guidance, strength, sanity, and the right ideal. **Clear Form Data**

Whom did I hurt? (1)	Where was I (2)	Did I arouse: (3)	Where was I at fault, what should I have done instead? (4)	Was each relation? (5)	Sex Prayer Page 69(6)	Sex Meditation Page 69(7)	The Earnest Prayers page 70
my spouse	Selfish: Dishonest: Inconsiderate:			S E L F I S H	*"God, please mold my ideals and help me to live up to them."* ☐	*"God, please show me what to do about this[each] specific matter"* ☐	We earnestly pray for: The right ideal Guidance in each questionable situation
my ex	Selfish: Dishonest: Inconsiderate:			S E L F I S H	*"God, please mold my ideals and help me to live up to them."* ☐	*"God, please show me what to do about this[each] specific matter"* ☐	Sanity The strength to do the right thing If sex is troublesome, we throw ourselves the harder into helping others.
my high school sweetheart	Selfish: Dishonest: Inconsiderate:			S E L F I S H	*"God, please mold my ideals and help me to live up to them."* ☐	*"God, please show me what to do about this[each] specific matter"* ☐	We think of their needs and work for them. This takes us out of ourselves. It quiets the imperious urge, when to yield would mean heartache.

THE BIG BOOK'S WAY TO "SENSIBLY OVERHAUL" OUR OWN SEX CONDUCT (Pages 68—70)

INSTRUCTIONS: a) Study from the bottom of page 68 to the end of third paragraph on page 70. **b)** Fill in Column 1from top to bottom. **c)** Do Column 2 **from top to bottom. d)** Fill in each of the remaining columns **from top to bottom.** *Do not work across the page from left to right.* Don't forget the **Sex Prayer** ("God, please mold my ideals and help me to live up to them") on page 69, and the Big Book's **Sex Meditation** ("God, please show me what to do about this [each] specific matter") on page 69. "The right answer will come if we want it". This will shape a "sane and sound ideal for our future sex life" (page 69). Be sure to restudy what happens if we "fall short of the chosen ideal and stumble" on page 70. Be sure to continue to pray the "Earnest" prayers from page 70 (on the right hand side of this page) for ongoing guidance, strength, sanity, and the right ideal. **Clear Form Data**

Whom did I hurt? (1)	Where was I (2)	Did I arouse: (3)	Where was I at fault, what should I have done instead? (4)	Was each relation? (5)	Sex Prayer Page 69(6)	Sex Meditation Page 69(7)	The Earnest Prayers page 70
my spouse	Selfish: wanted spouse to be different; want my way; want sex; want love Dishonest: can't change anyone but myself; made choice; haven't been honest about needs and problems; haven't love what there is to love Inconsiderate: thought of myself and not spouse; how spouse feels affects how I feel about myself	Jealousy? Suspicion? **Bitterness?**	should invest myself into relationship should think of spouse's needs and not mine should be honest and loving and caring should do more around the house should love myself so I can be loved	S E L F I S H (Yes) ~~No~~	*"God, please mold my ideals and help me to live up to them."* ☑	*"God, please show me what to do about this[each] specific matter"* ☑	We earnestly pray for: The right ideal Guidance in each questionable situation
my ex	Selfish: wanted what I wanted from the relationship; ate myself out of the relationships thought of myself only; denied sex because of anger Dishonest: blamed spouse for the bad relationship instead of myself; did not invest myself into relationship; denied sex Inconsiderate: thought only of myself; thought I could fix things; didn't think of ex's needs or desires	**Jealousy?** **Suspicion?** **Bitterness?**	should have invested more into the relationship	S E L F I S H (Yes) ~~No~~	*"God, please mold my ideals and help me to live up to them."* ☑	*"God, please show me what to do about this[each] specific matter"* ☑	Sanity The strength to do the right thing If sex is troublesome, we throw ourselves the harder into helping others.
my high school sweetheart	Selfish: wanted sex without committed relationship; thought only of my needs; used other to get peer respect Dishonest: did not tell sweetheart the truth; lied about other relationships; pretended to be interested in things just to get the relationship Inconsiderate: my sexual needs were foremost; used the other in many ways	**Jealousy?** Suspicion? **Bitterness?**	should not have entered into the relationship; or, once having entered into it and realized the imbalance of emotions, should have ended it honestly and with grace.	S E L F I S H (Yes) ~~No~~	*"God, please mold my ideals and help me to live up to them."* ☑	*"God, please show me what to do about this[each] specific matter"* ☑	We think of their needs and work for them. This takes us out of ourselves. It quiets the imperious urge, when to yield would mean heartache.

THE BIG BOOK'S WAY TO "SENSIBLY OVERHAUL" OUR OWN SEX CONDUCT (Pages 68—70)

INSTRUCTIONS: a) Study from the bottom of page 68 to the end of third paragraph on page 70. **b)** Fill in Column 1from top to bottom. **c)** Do Column 2 **from top to bottom. d)** Fill in each of the remaining columns **from top to bottom.** *Do not work across the page from left to right.* Don't forget the **Sex Prayer** ("God, please mold my ideals and help me to live up to them") on page 69, and the Big Book's **Sex Meditation** ("God, please show me what to do about this [each] specific matter") on page 69. "The right answer will come if we want it". This will shape a "sane and sound ideal for our future sex life" (page 69). Be sure to restudy what happens if we "fall short of the chosen ideal and stumble" on page 70. Be sure to continue to pray the "Earnest" prayers from page 70 (on the right hand side of this page) for ongoing guidance, strength, sanity, and the right ideal. **Clear Form Data**

Whom did I hurt? (1)	Where was I (2)	Did I arouse: (3)	Where was I at fault, what should I have done instead? (4)	Was each relation? (5)	Sex Prayer Page 69(6)	Sex Meditation Page 69(7)	The Earnest Prayers page 70
my spouse	Selfish: wanted spouse to be different; want my way; want sex; want love Dishonest: can't change anyone but myself; made choice; haven't been honest about needs and problems; haven't love what there is to love Inconsiderate: thought of myself and not spouse; how spouse feels affects how I feel about myself	Jealousy? Suspicion? Bitterness? x		S E L F I S H Yes No	*"God, please mold my ideals and help me to live up to them."* ☐	*"God, please show me what to do about this[each] specific matter"* ☐	We earnestly pray for: The right ideal Guidance in each questionable situation
my ex	Selfish: wanted what I wanted from the relationship; ate myself out of the relationships thought of myself only, denied sex because of anger Dishonest: blamed spouse for the bad relationship instead of myself; did not invest myself into relationship; denied sex Inconsiderate: thought only of myself; thought I could fix things; didn't think of ex's needs or desires	Jealousy? x Suspicion? x **Bitterness?** x		S E L F I S H Yes No	*"God, please mold my ideals and help me to live up to them."* ☐	*"God, please show me what to do about this[each] specific matter"* ☐	Sanity The strength to do the right thing If sex is troublesome, we throw ourselves the harder into helping others.
my high school sweetheart	Selfish: wanted sex without committed relationship; thought only of my needs; used other to get peer respect Dishonest: did not tell sweetheart the truth; lied about other relationships; pretended to be interested in things just to get the relationship Inconsiderate: my sexual needs were foremost; used the other in many ways	Jealousy? Suspicion? x **Bitterness?** x		S E L F I S H Yes No	*"God, please mold my ideals and help me to live up to them."* ☐	*"God, please show me what to do about this[each] specific matter"* ☐	We think of their needs and work for them. This takes us out of ourselves. It quiets the imperious urge, when to yield would mean heartache.

Clear Data

STEP EIGHT AND NINE LIST

This form is not taken in its entirety from the Big Book, but is a useful guide. Fill out the form directly from the saved copies of your Fourth Step Inventory worksheets. Complete all Amends marked in the "Now?" column. When done, move the items from the "Sometime?" column to "Now?" and the "Never!" items to "Sometime?" You'll find that the Nevers have turned into Sometimes, and the Sometimes into Nows. Continue this process until you complete all items on your Ninth Step.

Name of person harmed:	Harm done to that person:	Possible Amend(s) for that harm (Apology, Restitution, Public Acknowledgement, Living)	Will this Amend harm that person or anyone else?	Ready to do the Amend(s)... Now?	Some-time?	Never!
spouse	didn't invest in the relationship haven't been honest about my needs haven't been honest about my feelings having given spouse love required		Yes No	☐	☐	☐
person who hurt me as a child	have allowed that person to haunt my entire life have allowed that person to keep me from enjoying love haven't told anyone about what happened		Yes No	☐	☐	☐
ex	denied sex didn't invest in the relationship used ex		Yes No	☐	☐	☐
OA	don't contribute at meetings don't work the steps haven't recovered		Yes No	☐	☐	☐
my children	don't give them love haven't talked about my hurts and illness		Yes No	☐	☐	☐
people who are suffering	don't help them don't help any of them am paralyzed		Yes No	☐	☐	☐

Clear Data

STEP EIGHT AND NINE LIST

This form is not taken in its entirety from the Big Book, but is a useful guide. Fill out the form directly from the saved copies of your Fourth Step Inventory worksheets. Complete all Amends marked in the "Now?" column. When done, move the items from the "Sometime?" column to "Now?" and the "Never!" items to "Sometime?" You'll find that the Nevers have turned into Sometimes, and the Sometimes into Nows. Continue this process until you complete all items on your Ninth Step.

Name of person harmed:	Harm done to that person:	Possible Amend(s) for that harm (Apology, Restitution, Public Acknowledgement, Living)	Will this Amend harm that person or anyone else?	Ready to do the Amend(s)... Now?	Some-time?	Never!
spouse				☐	☐	☐
person who hurt me as a child				☐	☐	☐
ex				☐	☐	☐
OA				☐	☐	☐
my children				☐	☐	☐
people who are suffering				☐	☐	☐

Clear Data

STEP EIGHT AND NINE LIST

This form is not taken in its entirety from the Big Book, but is a useful guide. Fill out the form directly from the saved copies of your Fourth Step Inventory worksheets. Complete all Amends marked in the "Now?" column. When done, move the items from the "Sometime?" column to "Now?" and the "Never!" items to "Sometime?" You'll find that the Nevers have turned into Sometimes, and the Sometimes into Nows. Continue this process until you complete all items on your Ninth Step.

Name of person harmed:	Harm done to that person:	Possible Amend(s) for that harm (Apology, Restitution, Public Acknowledgement, Living)	Will this Amend harm that person or anyone else?	Ready to do the Amend(s)... Now?	Some-time?	Never!
spouse	didn't invest in the relationship haven't been honest about my needs haven't been honest about my feelings having given spouse love required	living amend honesty about needs and feelings give love and think of spouse's needs and desires	~~Yes~~ (No)	☐	☐	☐
person who hurt me as a child	have allowed that person to haunt my entire life have allowed that person to keep me from enjoying love haven't told anyone about what happened	tell my loved ones the truth about what happened to me kick that person out of my head understand how that person has become an un-human person who cannot know the joys that I am capable of feeling	~~Yes~~ (No)	☐	☐	☐
ex	denied sex didn't invest in the relationship used ex	apologize tell truth about cheating	(Yes) ~~No~~	☐	☐	☐
OA	don't contribute at meetings don't work the steps haven't recovered	work the steps and recover	~~Yes~~ (No)	☐	☐	☐
my children	don't give them love haven't talked about my hurts and illness	living amends give love tell them the truth	~~Yes~~ (No)	☐	☐	☐
people who are suffering	don't help them don't help any of them am paralyzed	help whom I can when I can stop being paralyzed	~~Yes~~ (No)	☐	☐	☐

Clear Data

STEP EIGHT AND NINE LIST

This form is not taken in its entirety from the Big Book, but is a useful guide. Fill out the form directly from the saved copies of your Fourth Step Inventory worksheets. Complete all Amends marked in the "Now?" column. When done, move the items from the "Sometime?" column to "Now?" and the "Never!" items to "Sometime?" You'll find that the Nevers have turned into Sometimes, and the Sometimes into Nows. Continue this process until you complete all items on your Ninth Step.

Name of person harmed:	Harm done to that person:	Possible Amend(s) for that harm (Apology, Restitution, Public Acknowledgement, Living)	Will this Amend harm that person or anyone else?	Ready to do the Amend(s)... Now?	Some-time?	Never!
spouse	didn't invest in the relationship haven't been honest about my needs haven't been honest about my feelings having given spouse love required	living amend honesty about needs and feelings give love and think of spouse's needs and desires	Yes No	☐	☐	☐
person who hurt me as a child	have allowed that person to haunt my entire life have allowed that person to keep me from enjoying love haven't told anyone about what happened	tell my loved ones the truth about what happened to me kick that person out of my head understand how that person has become an un-human person who cannot know the joys that I am capable of feeling	Yes No	☐	☐	☐
ex	denied sex didn't invest in the relationship used ex	apologize tell truth about cheating	Yes No	☐	☐	☐
OA	don't contribute at meetings don't work the steps haven't recovered	work the steps and recover	Yes No	☐	☐	☐
my children	don't give them love haven't talked about my hurts and illness	living amends give love tell them the truth	Yes No	☐	☐	☐
people who are suffering	don't help them don't help any of them am paralyzed	help whom I can when I can stop being paralyzed	Yes No	☐	☐	☐

Made in the USA
Las Vegas, NV
21 November 2024

12294572R00052